Praise for Kathleen Jamie

Winner of the
John Burroughs Medal • Costa Prize for Poetry
Orion Book Award • Forward Poetry Prize

"[Kathleen Jamie's] essays guide you softly along coastlines of varying continents, exploring caves, and pondering ice ages until the narrator stumbles over—not a rock on the trail, but mortality, maybe the earth's, maybe our own, pointing to new paths forward through the forest."
—Delia Owens, "By the Book" in *The New York Times Book Review*

"A sorceress of the essay form. Never exotic, down to earth, she renders the indefinable to the reader's ear. Hold her tangible words and they'll take you places."
—John Berger, author of *Ways of Seeing* and *About Looking*

"Whether she is addressing birds or rivers, or the need to accept loss, or, sometimes, the desire to escape our own lives, her work is earthy and rigorous, her language at once elemental and tender."   —2012 Costa Poetry Prize citation

"Kathleen Jamie is a supreme listener. . . . In the quietness of her listening, you hear her own voice: clear, subtle, respectful, and so unquenchably curious that it makes the world anew."
—Richard Mabey

"The leading Scottish poet of her generation."
—*The Sunday Times* (London)

Kathleen Jamie, one of the UK's foremost poets, is the author of four books of poetry and three nonfiction titles, including *Sightlines*. Her many honors include the 2017 Royal Geographic Society Ness Award, conferred upon Jamie "for outstanding creative writing at the confluence of travel, nature, and culture"; the 2013 Costa Poetry Book Award; and the Forward Poetry Prize of the Year. A professor of creative writing at the University of Stirling, she lives with her family in Fife, Scotland.

Surfacing

KATHLEEN JAMIE

PENGUIN BOOKS

PENGUIN BOOKS
An imprint of Penguin Random House LLC
penguinrandomhouse.com

First published in Great Britain by Sort Of Books 2019
Published in Penguin Books 2019

LIBRARY OF CONGRESS CATALOGING-IN-PUBLICATION DATA
Names: Jamie, Kathleen, 1962– author.
Title: Surfacing / Kathleen Jamie.
Description: New York : Penguin Books, 2019. | "First published
in Great Britain by Sort Of Books 2019"—Verso title page. |
Identifiers: LCCN 2019025260 (print) | LCCN 2019025261 (ebook) |
ISBN 9780143134459 (trade paperback) | ISBN 9780525506256 (ebook)
Subjects: LCSH: Jamie, Kathleen, 1962—Travel—Scotland. |
Jamie, Kathleen, 1962—Travel—Alaska. | Jamie, Kathleen,
1962—Travel—Tibet Autonomous Region (China) | Life change events. |
Scotland—Description and travel. | Alaska—Description and travel. |
Tibet Autonomous Region (China)—Description and travel.
Classification: LCC PR6060.A477 A6 2019 (print) |
LCC PR6060.A477 (ebook) | DDC 824/.914—dc23
LC record available at https://lccn.loc.gov/2019025260
LC ebook record available at https://lccn.loc.gov/2019025261

Printed in the United States of America
1 3 5 7 9 10 8 6 4 2

Set in Goudy Old Style

For Phil

Contents

The Reindeer Cave

You're sheltering in a cave, thinking about the Ice Age. From the cave-mouth: a West Highland landscape in spring, in the early Anthropocene. On the hillside opposite, six red deer have bedded down in the heather. It's raining, a soft Highland rain, a smirr.

Not half an hour ago, you were walking beside the burn in a narrow ravine further up the glen. You heard something, glanced up to see a large rock bounce then plummet into the burn twenty-five yards in front of you. The echo faded but your heart was still hammering as you backed away.

They call these caves the 'Bone Caves' because of all the animal bones found buried inside, animals long extinct in this country. You're in 'Reindeer Cave,' where antlers rather than bones were discovered. An excavation in the 1920s produced hundreds of reindeer antlers, almost all from females.

You sit at the cave-mouth, looking out at the rain, thinking about the Ice Age.

You realise you haven't a clue. We can wait, say the hills. Take your time.

The ice came and went, is that right? Ice covered the land and froze the sea for thousands of years, but now and again, every hundred thousand years or so, came milder spells when the ice retreated, tundra formed on the land and reindeer wandered in. Glaciers in the glens, or what became the glens.

To reach the caves, you climbed a grassy slope a hundred-and-fifty feet above the river. You try to imagine stepping from the cave-mouth onto ice and moraine.

Some years ago, cave-divers entered into this same hill by an entrance higher on the moor, by the back door, so to speak, intending to explore a system below the Bone Caves.

It makes you quail, the thought of crawling through darkness and passageways and underground streams. Echoes and falling rocks.

Deep within, the cavers found the bones of a bear. What was that like? Like reaching the memory of the hill itself.

Eventually, carefully, the bones were brought to the surface. In time they were carbon-dated. They were forty-five thousand years old. A long sleep, even for a bear: sixteen million days and nights had passed in the upper world. Long enough for the ice to return, then yield again, then return in one last snap, then leave for good – or at least for now.

The cave-mouth the bear must have used has since been blocked by the rocky detritus of that last ice-grip, the one which ended ten thousand years ago and created the land we know.

Ten thousand years – in the great scheme of things, we're living through a warm bank holiday weekend.

Warm and getting warmer.

As to the antlers, they were found before carbon-dating became available. Then, excited speculation concerned us, people, humans! Might there have been Paleolithic humans here, to gather up all those antlers and store them in a cave?

But there's no evidence for that. Female reindeer, caribou, shed their antlers naturally, up on the calving grounds, and some antlers must have fallen onto the glacier to be borne downhill and swilled into the cave-mouth by meltwater, and duly buried. That's the surmise.

The hoard of antlers is kept in the store of the National Museum of Scotland. They're not as you might imagine, not majestic. Ancient fragments, they look more like broken biscuits. Also in the store, wrapped in a box, are the bear bones, including the brown-stained skull. The skull was in the cave and what was in the skull? Bear mind, bear memory – when autumn came and the nights began to freeze, he remembered where the cave-mouth was, so he padded across the glacier.

Also stored away are the remains of other creatures of the caves – lynx, for example. Even the tiny bones of lemmings, saved for the nation in an old Cadbury's chocolate tin.

The world warms. Last winter was the wettest; no snow or ice to speak of, a flash of blue sky was rare as a comet, the nights were starless and lachrymose. The TV news showed floods and sandbags, householders weeping as they cleared the sodden mess. There were arguments about land management, flood-plains, deforestation. Commentators intoned, 'Is it climate change?'

Well, you thought sourly, if it walks like a duck and quacks like a duck, it's a duck.

D'où venons-nous? Que sommes-nous? Où allons-nous?

At your cave-mouth, you wonder if the ice will ever return, a natural cycle, or if we've gone too far with our Anthropocene. But who can answer that? We just can't grasp the scale of our species' effects. But the single falling stone which could smash our brains out – that we understand.

Now the rain's easing, and a small scruffy terrier appears at the cave-mouth. Following the dog come children. Their voices carry from down the slope: Daddy! Look! The caves!

A Reflection

ON A TRAIN, heading north. We'd crossed the Firth of Tay and stopped at the port city of Dundee, where the ship that took Scott to the Antarctic is berthed, and where oil rigs go to be repaired. Now we were out in the Angus countryside. Eastward, on the right, lay the North Sea but I was seated on the landward side where the view was of wintery fields.

The sea on one side, fields on the other. I'd been daydreaming, but came to my senses to notice that a shining spread of sea had appeared in my window, superimposed over the fields of brown earth. Then it vanished. A moment later it flashed back again, a stretch of sea, silvery over the land, but only for a few seconds. By now I was sitting up, interested in this phenomenon. The fields on the left gave way to pinewoods, the train tilted a little and, yes, the sea's reflection flashed on again, this time above the trees. If I narrowed my eyes I could see both sea and trees at once. And now there was a ship! A ghostly tanker was sailing over the pine trees.

There's an old ballad, isn't there? 'The False Bride.' 'How many strawberries grow in the salt sea? How many ships sail in the forest?'

A woman nearby was on her mobile, loud and getting louder. 'It's just so *stupid*. That's three times I've emailed her. They'll just *have to*.'

I watched the sea's reflection come and go until the train entered a cutting. When we emerged, the sea was gone. There were fields on the right, and from my side, the left, the distant Grampian hills with a dusting of fresh snow.

'I told her! I did! I told her!' The woman was still on her mobile. Her fellow passengers were glancing at each other, rolling their eyes.

There was 'The False Bride,' but the ship in the sky had caused something else to surface in my mind: it was an account William Scoresby had written. Scoresby was a whaling captain, and the son of a whaling captain. He had sailed north with his father every summer since he was twelve, and at the age of just twenty-one took command of his own ship, the *Baffin*. But slaughtering whales was a chore; Scoresby was much more interested in science and discovery. As he sailed north in 1822, he made maps and observations and detailed the strange Arctic phenomena he encountered off the eastern shores of Greenland. He wrote about snowflakes, refractions, rainbows and mirages.

On one July day, a beautifully fine one when the winds were light and the atmosphere highly refractive, Scoresby and his crew witnessed a marvel: two ships appeared, sailing upside down in the sky. He recognised the ships and knew them to be lying at least ten miles beyond sight. It happened again a fortnight later: in the crystalline light of an Arctic summer evening, the image of a ship appeared in the sky. It was inverted but so well defined he could pick out every sail. He pronounced it the *Fame*, his father's vessel, which at that moment lay well beyond the horizon. And so it proved to be.

How astonishing, to see what lay over the horizon.

My ship had been the right way up, sailing over trees.

'I know! I bloody know!' cried the woman on the phone. People had begun to glare at her by now.

We were heading for Aberdeen. Back then, the nineteenth century, if whalers and fishing boats put out of such ports, when they were gone they were gone. The whalers might be away for a year. A last message shouted from the gunwales of a northbound ship to a homebound one might be relayed eventually, perhaps to find itself overtaken by events. No sailor knew what he might find on his return. Nor did their wives know what happened once the ships slipped away. But the crewmen brought home souvenirs. The museums of the east coast all hold Inuit items, carried back here by whalers. The Arbuthnot Museum, in Peterhead, just two rooms above the public library, has in pride of place a stuffed polar bear, which had been brought home alive.

The polar bear has a stuffed musk-ox for company now, and a seal. There's a display case with a painted backdrop – a dramatic scene of a whaler held fast to towering ice, and its crew ashore, dancing around a bonfire. And in the case: a narwhal tusk, Inuit snowshoes, a dogwhip – things that fascinated Europeans. Another little cabinet held a delicate drawstring bag, just ten centimetres long, in pale, off-white Arctic colours. It had been fashioned from the webbed feet of a bird, perhaps a goose, and stitched so neatly that the claws become part of a pattern. Doubtless the Inuit maker knew what species of bird was best for the purpose, and how to catch one.

These Inuit things had been bartered for, the curator had said. 'Bartered for what?' I remember asking.

'Guns! And there were a lot of bairns born there, to Inuit women and brought up there, and the wives at home had no idea!'

False husbands, warmed by their icy fire.

I'd liked that museum, with its Inuit objects and polar bear. There were model fishing boats too, with names like *Fruitful Bough* and *Whinny Fold*, as if they did indeed sail in a forest.

Mary Scoresby died during her husband's Greenland voyage, the one when he'd seen ships in the sky. He didn't learn that truth until September, when he turned the *Baffin* home into the Mersey. There was something about a little boat making its way out toward his vessel, lowering its sail as it neared, the silence of its passengers, his friends.

The woman had ended her call at last. What had she known?

Now the North Sea was again visible on the right, with several ships riding at anchor, ships concerned with the oil rigs that lay over the horizon. I looked at once for their reflections, but it was noon, the light had changed.

In Quinhagak

TAKE AN ATLAS, or better a globe, and find the line that marks sixty degrees of latitude, then follow it west. If you begin in Shetland, you're at once swinging out over the North Atlantic. You snip off the last few miles of Cape Farewell, Greenland, make landfall in Labrador but soon launch out over Hudson's Bay. Keep going. The line demarks the northern border of Manitoba, Saskatchewan, Alberta and British Columbia. Keep going. Now you're in Alaska. Don't stop until the line at last reaches the Bering Sea. Now stop. Cross the sea and you'll be in Russia, beginning the long road home.

For the final hundred miles of Alaska, the imaginary line passes over the Kuskokwim–Yukon delta. The atlas will show no roads, just green scribbly waterways and melt-pools. The village of Quinhagak is right on this coast, tucked just under that sixty-degree line, just where the Kanektok River pours into the Bering Sea. In summer, that is. In winter the rivers freeze and snow falls deep.

Around seven hundred people live in the village, almost all of them Yup'ik. Their river, the Kanektok, is a noted salmon river. 'Kanektok' means 'New River Channel.' The rivers change course readily, in this watery world.

In summer, when the land is thawed, the only way to get there is by plane. Every coastal village has an airstrip. You can fly from Anchorage to the town of Bethel, the regional hub on the Kuskokwim River. From Bethel, six-seater planes skip back and forth to Goodnews Bay and Platinum, Sleetmute and Pilot Station, Russian Mission, Kongiganak, Quinhagak, Eek. In the aerial photographs that decorate the airport waiting room, these villages all look much the same: each photo features a braiding river with boats drawn up on muddy banks, and a straggle of small homes along a dirt road that begins and ends in tundra.

I arrived in Bethel in late July. The airport had the atmosphere of a busy provincial bus station. Almost everyone in the waiting room was Yup'ik; there was lots of meeting and greeting by dark-haired, softly spoken people who wore sweatpants and hoodies. Infants played on the floor, teenagers slept on benches. The bush pilots were mostly white, young and louche-looking. They wore overalls or fatigues. When a plane was ready to go, its pilot would appear at the door and call the name of the village destination, then lead his or her passengers across the tarmac. Sometimes a pilot went and shook a sleeping teenager. 'Hey, you going Eek?'

At Bethel I was nervous, jet-lagged, afraid I'd miss the plane; afraid I'd mishear 'Quinhagak' for 'Kongiganak' and end up there instead. 'Quinhagak' is pronounced 'Quin-ah-hawk' and, though I did my best, 'Huh,' its people chided me later. 'You say it like a white.' In Bethel also, I learned the phrase 'weather hold.' Fog over the delta means no flights and for some hours that morning the cloud rolled in from the coast. When it lifted, and flights resumed, a pilot duly appeared in the doorway and called out 'Quinhagak!' Three people walked out with her across the tarmac and climbed into the tiny plane.

'You the new teacher?' one of them asked me, a soft-spoken Yup'ik woman with a shopping bag. 'No? We're expecting a new teacher.'

The other was a white man, an electrician going out to do a little work on a new school, and, he said, a lot of fishing.

The pilot had long red hair tied in a loose bun with a biro stuck through it. In the plane she readied herself, then half turned in her seat.

'You guys definitely going Quinhagak? Just checking! Okay. There's emergency supplies in the back.'

The plane shuddered into life, rolled along, took off and immediately we were soaring over miles of emerald green and moss green, yellowish patches with coppery tints, here and there a smudge of purple, which was fireweed. Below the shuddering wing I saw narrow rivers with gravel banks lined by willows, melt-pools and creeks. At seven hundred feet we were low enough to see a line of moose tracks traversing a mudbank. Two white dabs were tundra swans. We flew over expanses of grey moss. When the plane tilted, and the horizon reared at the window, I saw the most flat and uninhabited landscape I had ever beheld.

The delta was barely a landscape at all; more like a waterscape into which some land had been released. Or land, through which water has been introduced, enough to make the land appear to float. It was both at once, a visual pun. A cold draught, worryingly cold, found its way in through the door at my elbow; the whole plane seemed to shiver. I looked down past the wing, hoping there might be animals down there. Caribou. Wolves.

After forty minutes the light ahead brightened as we neared the sea, and the village appeared as a prickle of telegraph poles, a telecoms mast, three wind turbines. Then we were descending, then bumping along a gravel-topped airstrip that appeared to be in the middle of nowhere.

When the propeller had whined down, the pilot jumped out to open our door. I clambered down onto the gravel, only slightly queasy. It was mid-afternoon, and silent. There seemed to be nothing and no one around but a lonely shed, and a sign which read 'Quinhagak – elevation 35 feet.' The light cascaded down from the whole sky. A ravishing, energising light.

* * *

For some time before this, years actually, whenever the chance arose, I'd been poking around museums on the east coast of the UK, looking at Inuit articles. If I found myself in Whitby, Dundee, Aberdeen, Peterhead, Stromness – wherever the nineteenth-century whaling ships sailed from, heading for the northern ice – I'd look in the local museum. Often enough, for good or ill, the whalers made contact with Inuit people, and bartered for curiosities to bring home. Not only objects – more than one live polar bear travelled south, and even Inuit people, persuaded or in some cases abducted. In Stromness there are snow goggles, and amulets in the shape of seals. In Aberdeen there are actual sealskin kayaks, slender and responsive. So much wit and knowing in the materials, and all the materials are natural, of course. I like them because they suggest a powerful relationship with the non-human world.

In Aberdeen University's museum I met a young curator called Jenny Downes and she went one step further. She said, if you're interested in Arctic or sub-Arctic artefacts, you ought to meet Rick Knecht. He's an archaeologist. He's working on a Yup'ik site in Alaska.

I had never heard the name 'Yup'ik' before. 'Inuit,' yes. 'Iñupiat,' almost. But not 'Yup'ik.' All are indigenous peoples of the circumpolar north.

Yes, said Jenny. You should meet Rick.

It was a sort of blind date. When I returned to Aberdeen, there was no mistaking Dr Knecht in the university foyer. Spot the Alaskan. Rick was sixty, burly, bearish, with a bushy grey beard; he wore baggy pants and a thick-checked shirt with a fisherman's waistcoat. When he spoke I had to listen hard, not least because of the place names, strange to me, but also because he's a bit shy at first and tends to mumble into his beard. It was Rick who told me about Quinhagak, the village and its river, and its extraordinary archaeological site. The site is called Nunallaq. ('Huh?' its people would chide me later. 'Try again.' The double 'll' is in the Welsh manner, or a Scots 'ch.' The 'q' resembles the cluck of a contented hen.) 'Nunallaq' simply means 'Old Village.' It teeters at the edge of the tundra a couple of miles down the beach from the modern village.

Rick showed me photographs. The beach is a straight, mile-long strip of dark sand. Facing the sea is a wall of tundra just two or three metres high. Because sea levels are rising fast, this tundra is eroding quickly; every day clods of earth and vegetation fall to the sand to be washed away. And, because the permafrost is melting, the land is losing its grip on itself, the more ready to surrender to the sea.

It was the sea, pawing at this wall of tundra, which exposed the buried village. The Quinhagak people had learned that, if they came to this part of the beach, they'd likely find artefacts freshly tumbled out of the earth: line weights, harpoon heads, jewellery, wooden arrow-shafts, fishing weights, darts, models of animals, even ceremonial dance-masks, ritually broken after use. All made by knowing hands from caribou antler, wood, stone, walrus ivory, grass. For generations the frozen earth had held these objects fast, like charms in a Christmas cake, but now the objects were falling to the seashore to be washed away for good.

The people knew what they were finding. They were Yup'ik things, their own ancestors' tools and adornments from pre-contact times, before Europeans arrived, before Christian missionaries came sailing upriver. Although the Nunallaq village site is only five hundred years old, it represents a time when the Yup'ik were hunter-gatherers and fended for themselves, when they did just fine.

So much was being lost that heartfelt, difficult conversations ensued among elders and community leaders. Some folk refused point blank to interfere with the dead and the possessions of the dead. Others implored. Please, they said. It's for the young. The young know nothing about their Yup'ik culture, their own inheritance. Please let us call in archaeologists, before it's too late. We know an archaeologist who will help.

Before he came to Scotland, Rick had lived in Alaska for thirty years. He was the founding director of the Alutiiq Museum and Repository in Kodiak, and founding director of the Museum of the Aleutians in Unalaska. And now he was teaching in Scotland. By the time we met, the dig was in its fifth season, and all the finds that had come out of the site were stored in Aberdeen. Everything, even the mud, airfreighted halfway round the world.

In a room at the end of a university corridor, Rick began opening fridges, cupboards and drawers. He showed me labrets, huge plugs that men wore in their lips or cheeks, and a multitude of 'dolls' – flat sticks with faces carved on, just three lines that could express everything from merriment to agony.

Rick said, 'Sometimes you're cleaning a stick and you turn it over and whoa! there's a face looking at you. Real subtle, like someone hiding in the woods.'

Not that they had woods there on the delta. Only driftwood, washed ashore or borne downriver from the interior. And no metal. Although the new site was only five hundred years old, it revealed a hunter-gatherer culture, a survival of the Paleolithic.

He told me that the dig was revitalising traditional skills which had been lost, that local people were so interested in the rediscovered artefacts that they were making replicas, and that meant relearning old techniques – ivory carving, for example. That was the point. Although the dig had turned out to be rich beyond imagining, it wasn't a treasure hunt; it was rebuilding a whole culture lost to colonialism, to missionary zeal.

Excavation could only take place across the short, bug-ridden weeks of high summer, when the land thawed. It had a few more years left to run before the funding expired. For now, the finds were here in Aberdeen, to be cleaned, preserved and catalogued. Some were being researched by PhD students.

At the end of the excavation, however, there would be a great return. All the thousands of artefacts would go home to the Yup'ik land where they belonged, legally and morally. They must and would go home. But, before that could happen, there had to be a place there to receive them, a museum or repository. That was a challenge. Quinhagak was a Yup'ik village, and not blessed with museum-quality buildings.

I saw more photos, this time of rain-soaked archaeologists, both white and Yup'ik, smiling as they held out the latest finds in muddy hands. They were all volunteers, students mostly, who had been promised 'an archaeological adventure by the Bering Sea'. The students saved their money and made the trip, about a dozen or fifteen of them at a time. The photographs showed the sea shining in the background. Or tundra – miles of it. Miles on miles.

That night I took the train home again. They filled my mind, these Yup'ik objects. The dig was revitalising a damaged culture, Rick had said. Developing resilience and confidence, he'd said.

At home I pulled out the atlas, found the sixty degree line, followed it a long way west. Then I emailed. Could I go? If I paid my way, like the students? Maybe write something about it, this place I've never heard of, this archaeological adventure by the Bering Sea?

* * *

The ravishing light. I shielded my jet-lagged eyes and saw a grey beat-up minibus driving onto the runway. Soon, we three passengers were ushered into it. The driver of the minibus was called Darren. Darren's accent was American, but not quite, there was a slowness to it. He said, yes he'd always lived here, and would never move.

'It's peaceful. We got everything we need.'

On the left from the bus windows, I saw faraway mountains. On the right we passed a lopsided shed with a broken-down lorry outside. Darren drove around potholes, then came the first pitched-roofed cabins, up on stilts. Everything in the village looked like it had been built in the last twenty-five years. Tatty, untidy, but newish.

'How long has the village been here, Darren?'

'Well,' said Darren, 'we don't know much about our ancestors. But the elders say there's been a settlement here for thousands of years. Why go anywhere else?'

'I remember,' he went on, 'when I was young, an elder saying – Why go anyplace? We got what we need here. Living off the land. We've got the river, salmon, trout. Fresh water ... but winter was bad.'

'Bad, meaning...?'

'No snow. We were travelling in boats and four-wheelers all winter. Same last year too. And then April, May, June were too hot.'

The woman agreed.

'There were fires out on the tundra,' she said.

'Yeah, the tundra was so dry. Then lightning! We had a lot of lightning. The lightning set the tundra on fire.'

'That's not common?' I asked.

'Not common. The smoke, the fumes was getting bad.'

We made one turn into a grey gravel road lined by tilting telegraph poles that cast wires forward and back. Towards us came four-wheelers, driven at speed by dark-haired, windswept drivers. The road passed cabins raised on stilts, and soon we stopped to set down my fellow passenger, the woman who had flown across the tundra with nothing more than a shy smile and a shopping bag. Her house was one of these weather-blasted cabins, raised up with stairs to the entrance. Every cabin seemed scoured and broken-paned, which shows what winter does. Were it not for the glorious light, it would have been dismal.

At a big school that was part building site, the electrician got out and said goodbye.

'You with the archaeologists?' asked Darren. 'I'll take you to the red building.'

He stopped in front of a big metal-clad hangar. It too was jacked up on wooden stilts. A ramp and stairs led up to its doors. The building was indeed rust red, except for a blue sign high on its wall which read 'Qanirtuuq Incorporated, Quinhagak, Alaska' with a logo which showed a circle quartered by crossed harpoons. Each quarter showed a different creature: seal, salmon, caribou, bear.

A huge, red, windowless shed.

'Is this it?' I said.

'Yeah, you just go right on up.'

I made to cross the road but stopped quick because a four-wheeler was racing along with a whole family aboard: mum, several kids and granny. Granny was being towed in a trailer, reclining on a sort of chaise longue. She was wearing a purple anorak, a purple knitted hat and shades. Everyone clasped a plastic tub, and a dog ran panting along behind. It was summer, berry-picking time, so Rick had said. Hence the tubs. The driver waved, and I waved back.

* * *

Soon I learned that this 'red building,' where Darren had left me, had been the supermarket before a newer, even bigger one was built nearby. I don't know if I expected the village to have a supermarket, but I was making an effort not to expect anything. The red building was now the village hall, but for the high summer weeks of the dig the Quinhagak people, via the village council, hand it over to the archaeologists for use as a base camp, refectory, social hub, laboratory. The building was white inside, and because there were no windows electric strip lights were always switched on. In there, you could almost forget about the sky and sunlight and tundra outside.

In the body of the room were set out two long plastic-topped trestle tables. On every horizontal surface, a laptop was being charged. There was Wi-Fi, Facebook. Wooden trays of bones and sticks lay on the floor to dry.

A grocery store. Wi-Fi. I was beginning to hear Rick's droll humour in his phrase 'Alaskan wilderness.' There was even a cook, thank god, the calm and cheerful Cheryl, whose domain was a stove and some worktops, and couple of huge fridge-freezers. Her job was to turn out breakfast and evening meals for the two dozen archaeologists and hangers-on like myself. Every morning I'd hear her on her cell phone, calling heaven knows where to have supplies flown in.

Because I'd arrived mid-afternoon, and everyone else was down on site and wouldn't be back for hours, it was Cheryl who greeted me and showed me where I'd sleep. A dash back across the road from the red building stood a grey Quonset hut, which is an American Nissen hut. It had been fitted out with rooms off a corridor, each with bunk beds roughly knocked together out of two-by-fours. It got filthy with mud from the site and the sanitation was limited – the village was in the midst of installing a piped water and sewerage system. But Rick told me later the Quonset hut was far better than the tents the diggers had had to use for the first couple of seasons, at the edge of town, what with the bugs and bears.

Again, electric lights burned all day. But in the corridor of the Quonset hut was a wolf-skin, draped over a sack barrow. Its fur was thick, pale honey-coloured. The moment Cheryl left me, I thrust my hand into the wolf-fur and my hand immediately began to warm. I lifted the pelt and smelled it. The wolf's muzzle was intact, pointed like a mask. One could wear it, and look out at the world through a wolf's eyes. That was tempting. A sign of the surrounding wild.

The diggers work long days, taking advantage of the midsummer light. It was past seven o'clock before a beat-up yellow station wagon and a couple of four-wheelers brought the crew home. Two dozen muddy youngsters discharged themselves up the stairs and into the red building, bringing chatter and mud and bucketsful of earth and wood and all the day's finds. An excited puppy gambolled amongst them but was soon ejected, for fear he'd chew the old bones.

I'd met Rick several times since that first winter afternoon in Aberdeen and here he was, in his element. Melia his wife was here too. Melia is herself a museum curator in Aberdeen but she was taking a busman's holiday, joining Rick on site and assisting with the finds.

No one had imagined how many finds there would be at Nunallaq, how much cataloguing and preserving would be required. I was glad to see Melia. She is a few years younger than her husband, and a good naturalist. Another Alaskan, when they met she was working in a fish canning factory, but they discovered a shared love for archaeology. It was she who had taken me under her wing when I had determined to come to Quinhagak. She was small and bustling, happy in the backwoods.

Melia had brought her telescope, and on my first evening she offered to walk with me through the village and down to the river to look for birds. I wondered at first if it was alright for us, strangers and non-Yu'pik, to ramble about the village like this, but everyone knew the archaeologists were in town. People smiled and the umpteen dogs all seemed friendly enough.

We walked the few gravel-topped streets. Between the cabins were sheds, wrecked snowmobiles, driftwood, sometimes garbage, sometimes whalebones, empty lots with stagnant water and trash, grasses and wildflowers. As we went, Melia explained about the stilts, which made the buildings look skittish, and all the junk: it was because of permafrost. Nothing could be buried. Even the shiny new sewage pipes were propped above ground, and insulated to keep their heat in. If a warm structure lay in direct contact with the ground, the ground would soon melt and heave, causing the structure to collapse.

As for the junk, there was nowhere for anything to go. 'Landfill' is impossible. The wrecked snowmachines and oil drums, discarded bikes and satellite dishes stay just where they are. If they get buried at all, it's by snow.

A man in a singlet was sitting up on his doorstep, smoking a cigarette. As we passed, he pointed to the telescope and called, 'You bird-lovers? Huh, I'm a bird-killer! A hunter, yeah. But d'you know the best thing in my life? My grandchildren, yeah.'

* * *

The next morning, as on every morning bar Sundays, the team took their filthy outdoor clothes and their packed lunches and climbed into a yellow pick-up truck. Rick drove, taking the one road, gravel-topped, which swung out of town and followed the coast for a couple of miles before it petered out. It passed under three wind turbines and a telecoms mast. Often we'd see short-eared owls hunting over the verges, and loons passing overhead, arrow-straight, bearing fish toward their young.

It wasn't quite true that the town's junk had nowhere to go: there was a scrapyard/garbage site at the edge of town where a chain-link fence surrounded a fire-pit: a thin, constant plume of smoke dispersed over the land. There were always ravens perched on the wire, like janitors. That was where we parked to reach the site.

Of course, the scrapyard joke wasn't lost on the archaeologists. Come back in five hundred years, and we'll be digging these beauties out of the mud. Look! A twentieth-century fridge! A bicycle wheel! But it's a hollow joke: the rate the coastline is eroding, the dump won't be there in five hundred years, or even fifty. Soon, the Bering Sea will be dealing with the crumpled firetruck and smashed windscreens.

But such was the daily commute to work: the diggers would spill out of the wagon to jump tussock to tussock a quarter-mile down to the shore. Underfoot it was boggy, with patches of caribou moss and salmonberry and the herby-smelling 'Labrador tea,' which is like a spruce tree three inches tall.

The first day, Rick gave me a short tour. On the edge of the tundra a semi-subterranean settlement was being excavated, or what was left of it, much having already been washed away. From the landward side there appeared to be an entranceway with logs laid like a boardwalk, and from that central alley, which would have been low and covered, there opened dwellings or work areas, all half-underground. Nunallaq would have been a winter home, because for the rest of the year people dispersed to camps, for fishing or hunting. A semi-subterranean alleyway, with rooms or houses off.

'Like at Skara Brae?' I asked.

'Yes, like at Skara Brae. Or like a cheapo motel!'

Except here, there was no stone to build with. Here, people used sods cut from the tundra for their walls, and driftwood logs to support the roof. The sod-wall houses had long collapsed; they were now just lumps of compressed earth.

Rick handed me over to Veronique Forbes, a delightful French Canadian and one of the site's assistant field directors, who gave me a job and instructions. I was to fetch a trowel, dustpan and bucket from a large tent, and a pad to kneel on, and take a place at a sod-wall. Vero, her face half wrapped in a bandana against the bugs, wanted the wall removed to expose the hard-packed floor which appeared to run underneath.

'You see how this floor comes? Take away this wall down to there.'

'Take it away?' I asked.

'Yes, just take it away.'

At first I pussyfooted with the trowel, but there was no need to be too careful, not here. Vero came back to check my progress and laughed. 'Just scrape quick,' she said, in her singing accent. 'Take it down.' If we didn't take it, the sea soon would.

So we worked, bent figures in the mud. If the blackfly became intolerable, huge electric fans were produced and hooked up to a generator, to try to blow them away.

The major find that day was a bentwood bowl, almost complete. Carefully excavated, it looked as if you could just lift it away, but at a half-metre down its base was still frozen in place. It was photographed, then just left for an hour or two, till the sun melted the ice.

In the early years of the dig, the ice was only ten centimetres under the surface of the land. Now it is half a metre. Only six years before, when the dig began, everyone had had to wrap up in layers against the cold. Bring thermals! I was told. Bring longjohns! But my cold-weather gear came home unused. 'It's like the site's been towed five hundred miles south', said Rick, 'in just five years.'

The landscape was astonishing. There was nothing I wanted to do more than sit quietly and look at it, come to terms with its vastness. At lunchtime, while the others ate in the mess tent, I wandered along the beach a short distance away from the site and sat on a clump of earth new-fallen from the tundra. The sand was damp and dark grey, but the sea had vanished. In its stead lay a silent, shining realm. Almost to the horizon, and for miles north and south, lay silver mudflats, with the sky reflected in shallow pools. The sky held every sort of cloud, every season, and through gaps in the cloud a dreamy turquoise I'd never seen before.

I hadn't imagined it would be silent. Before I came I'd imagined waves and rocks, like the coast of north-west Scotland, tides and wind. Not this silver and silent reach. There were phantasms out there: wavering and floating forms. A flock of small waders flew low over the mudflats, settled again. Through binoculars, I saw a crimped edge on the horizon, which might have been waves.

Sea, and land. Southward, it might have been miles away, a long spit of land reached out to sea, mere brushstrokes of greens with hints of fawn. Further yet, a range of mountains, just visible through a haze. On the spit, however, a shape caught my eye and, having seen it, I couldn't not look, because I was certain it was a living creature.

In a place with no rocks and no trees, the shape sat squarish, dark, prominent.

I stood on top of the clump of earth and trained the binoculars. Even so, the animal was at the edge of my vision. How many miles away, I couldn't say. Now I was fixated, waiting for the moment the creature moved and revealed its nature. It could be a woman picking berries, as it was berry season. Perhaps even a bear. We had been warned against walking down that way, alone. They kept a gun at the site, just in case. I wanted this distant creature to be a bear. It was surely large enough. A bear eating berries on the tundra – how thrilling! I watched till my eyes strained. But then, after long minutes, my woman-or-bear spread two black wings and took to the air. A raven! A raven, visible as an event on the landscape. I laughed at myself. Clearly, there was work to do with scale. One had to make allowances for this extraordinary light. But then again, maybe it showed how readily, in this unfixed place, the visible shifts. Transformation is possible. A bear can become a bird. A sea can vanish, rivers change course. The past can spill out of the earth, become the present.

* * *

Back at the site the team was again at work. There was a general muddiness, a hum of good-natured conversation. Rick was making his way around the perimeter path toward the finds tent. As he passed, he showed me what he was going to record: a slender wooden dart with a tip of bird-bone, the length of his mud-stained hand.

My own role being unfixed, I could spend my time digging at the site or not as I pleased. I could go to work

for the morning, or help in the red building, scrubbing
tables mostly, or ramble about the village, dodging the
four-wheelers. People greeted me with a wave or a few
words, no less and no more. Often I wondered about
the cabins up on stilts, what they were like inside.
Their owners were clearly hunters: there were sealskins
stretched to dry on an outhouse wall, and rows of little
desiccated corpses, ground squirrels, pegged like socks
on a line.

Hunter-gatherers with a grocery store. I went in there,
also, to drift in fascination down its American aisles.
Pop-Tarts, pizza, a few wilting cabbages. There were
even coconuts, flown across the tundra in the shuddering
plane. But no booze. Quinhagak is a dry village. We'd
all been warned against bringing any. 'Alcohol use has
contributed to more death and injury in rural Alaska
than bears, cold water and weather combined. Because
of this we must have a zero tolerance policy regarding
alcohol. *If you violate this policy you will be sent home on
the next plane.*'

One evening soon after I'd arrived, still jet-lagged, I
was sitting on the steps of the Quonset hut watching this
new world, when a terrible siren began to wail. I stood,
alarmed, looking round. Not an air raid. Not even an
ambulance – where would an ambulance go? The siren
wailed, and then a male voice called through a loud-
hailer. 'Time to go home! Time to stop playing!'

It was the Community Safety Officer, all dressed in
black, mounted on his four-wheeler, patrolling the few
streets. 'Time to go home now!'

Ten p.m., curfew time for children. But it was still light, and summer is so short. Who would want to go in, when you could play outdoors in the gloaming, as my pals and I used to, long ago?

But the next day was a school day, and also there are bears out there in the night. Hadn't the villagers shot one earlier in the year, for hanging round the town too persistently? And here was the Community Safety Officer, a sort of Wee Willie Winkie, running through the town.

* * *

In due course, the plane brought home Warren Jones. He'd been in Las Vegas. Warren was the president of the Village Corporation. The Corporation owned the grocery store, the hardware store, the fuel store. The Corporation owned the land. Almost everyone held shares in the Corporation; therefore the people owned the land.

I'd been told: you want something done, you ask Warren Jones. In his forties, he was bigger built than most Yup'ik men and often wore a black bomber jacket with the Corporation's logo on the back. If he seemed a bit brusque, it was because no one knew the pressures of maintaining a sober and functional village community better than he did. Hence the annual Las Vegas tip, to blow off steam.

Warren was one of those most supportive of the dig, who'd argued passionately for it, and had called

Rick when given the go-ahead. They worked closely together, dealing with sensitivities and politics, the sheer unexpected scale of the thing.

One morning when the others had gone to the site, I stayed behind and in due course traipsed upstairs myself and found Warren at a desk strewn with papers and invoices. There were windows up here: his office gave a view of a silent square of tundra.

I introduced myself, and said I was a writer and that I'd like, if possible, to learn something about Yup'ik life, but even as I said it, it sounded lame. Yup'ik life was all around me. The river and the land, the tatty cabins, the constant four-wheelers, the birds and berries, the matriarch in a florid *kuspuk* I'd overheard on her cellphone: 'Yeah, but she's *family*. You gotta look after your *family*.'

Warren gazed out of the window. Had he heard this before? Of course. They'd had long, long years of Europeans colonising and disparaging their 'savage' life, then suddenly here we were supplicating, marvelling at their relationship with nature, the last of the hunter-gatherers.

'Just tell 'em we don't live in igloos.'

'I will.'

'In Vegas they said – hey, don't you guys live in igloos?'

'I'll tell them. I heard you had a mild winter?'

'What winter? Last year, you could hit through the river-ice with just two blows. We couldn't go anyplace.'

Warren spoke about the dig. 'We pleaded with those elders. We said it was for the youngsters. How are they to know their own culture? We had *nothing*. When I was growing up, all we got was the church! We knew *nothing* about our own culture.'

'And is it working?'

Warren relaxed as he spoke.

'It's pivotal. Last year we held a dance. The dig inspired it. Did you know that? On that site, they are discovering dance-masks that our ancestors wore. The missionaries told us our ceremonies were devil worship! They brainwashed us! There hadn't been a ceremonial dance in this village for a hundred years. Well, one of the teachers put this dance together from elders' memories and fragments from other villages. They made that dance and the youngsters performed it.'

He looked defiant. 'Well, the first time that drum hit, the hair on my neck stood up. I thought, *It's back!* Now, I'm telling the hunters to keep the wattles of the caribou. It's what the women's dance-fans are made of. Now they are required again, for the first time in a hundred years.'

'That's thrilling.' I said.

'They had stopped it. The church. They said it was devil worship!'

'Do you think fortunes have changed? In the village?'

Warren nodded.

'To do with this dig?'

'Other villages are watching. We can show them how. There's a lot of sites out there...'

'Did you ever imagine how big it would become, how important...?'

This time he slowly shook his head, his eyes wide.

He said, 'You know we do the "show and tell," at the end of the season? First time, forty people came. Last year, it was eighty. This time we've got TV reporters coming, *National Geographic* are sending people... Since this dig began, kids from this village are hunting, carving again. They're working on the dig, learning archaeology, learning their own traditions. We're sending more kids to college. Is that a coincidence? I don't think so.'

* * *

Beyond the village, north and east and south, there was always the alluring tundra. Any offshore breeze brought a fragile summer scent; for miles inland grasses shivered. I could scan the land with my binoculars – a pile of old pallets behind the grocery store made a good vantage point. Small flocks of birds passed over with piping notes, to hide themselves in far-off waterways. But you couldn't just strike off. You'd get lost in its hidden marshes and pools. Everyone said so. And there were bears, of course, a lot this year.

One day, the team found fresh prints on the sand just below the site. Had a bear passed by while they were all at work? 'No,' said Melia. 'We'd have smelled it. Bears stink. It must have come in the night.'

On site, I came to enjoy screening. If you were working half a metre below ground level, you could almost forget there was a world beyond the site. A bear could pass unseen, if not unsmelled. Up at the screens, however, you were elevated. The screens were wire sieves, like waist-high tables, perched on top of the spoil heaps on the edge of the site; it was earth worked through the screens that formed the heaps.

As the heaps grew, so the screens were raised ever higher; they now stood at a commanding seven or eight feet. On site, you trowelled the thick damp earth, dumped the spoil in buckets, then you had to haul your heavy buckets up the heap and tip the contents onto the screen, then work it with your trowel again, back and forth, checking for any small artefacts which had been missed. It happened: amber beads, carvings, flat sticks marked with smiling or scowling faces had all been found in the screens. Many objects had faces marked on them. Some, Rick said, showed the spirit of the thing looking out at our world. They didn't seem to like what they saw.

You could choose to work facing the sea or you could face inland. You could watch for birds – now and again a short-eared owl would fly low over the vegetation with deeply beating, slightly nervous wings. Sometimes harriers, hunting. You could see forever landward or seaward. But also they were sociable places. In the time it took to screen a couple of buckets, you could have a proper conversation with your neighbour, as your trowels rasped against the wire mesh.

That was how I met Mike Smith, a likeable young man of twenty or twenty-one, born and raised in Quinhagak. Mike had a day job with the tribal council,

but he came down to the site when he could, battering
along the beach on a four-wheeler. He had the Yup'ik
round face and black hair, the makings of a goatee
beard, a gap-tooth grin. He often wore shades and a
beanie hat. Some of the local folk seemed reticent, but
Mike enjoyed the summer influx of the outside world to
Quinhagak, part of the seasonal round.

We coincided at the screens soon after I'd arrived and
we spoke about the land. Eastward stretched thirty, forty
miles of tundra, in shades of russet, green and fawn, then
a rim of mountains. The vast sky, hosting every species of
cloud. Mike said, 'The bog cotton is abundant this year.
We say when that happens, there will be bears around.
Don't know why, there just are. And it's true: there are
more bears this year. Also, when the bog-cotton seeds
blow away, then the salmonberries are ripe. You don't
have to go look.'

'It's some landscape...' I said.

He laughed. 'It's my refrigerator!'

'Do you go hunting?'

'Sure.'

I asked Mike to tell me the story of the site.

Though the village had been lost and buried, its story
had survived. For five hundred years there had been
handed down a story about an abandoned village, though
no one knew where it was.

He paused for a moment or two, trowel in hand.
'Okay. This is the story I heard as a child. The story of
the abducted woman. There was a woman, and she was
out upriver. She came from another village up there,

and some men from this village here caught her and abducted her, and brought her back here to be a slave. But, while she was here, she overheard them plotting. The men from this village were plotting an attack on her hometown. So she managed to escape and she made her way home again, across the tundra and rivers. It would have taken some days, probably. Two days, maybe four days. When she got home, she told what she had heard. So the men of her hometown decided to attack first. The hunters and the warriors got together and came down here, they came down on kayaks on the tide – you've seen how fast the tide comes in. They surprised the people here...'

He paused. 'Yeah. That was the story that we told, and then we found this site.'

He paused again. 'That was back in the "bow and arrow wars." They fired in burning arrows and set this village alight. They set this village alight and when the people came out choking, they killed them.'

We scraped on through the mud.

'I don't get war, me,' said Mike. 'But this dig is *interesting*.'

When I'd screened both bucketloads, I looked out again at the mountains. The light was always shifting there, throwing some ravines and corries into shade, picking out distant summits. The 'bow and arrow wars' had happened five hundred years ago during the Little Ice Age. There was famine and want enough in Europe; here it must have been desperate.

Mike followed my gaze.

'That's where the wolves are!' he grinned.

* * *

There was one track down to the river where I could go alone without fear of bears and often did. It was right down at the estuary, and it served four or five old-looking houses. The very last dwelling had a roof of corrugated iron, painted in three vertical bands like a flag. I thought of it as a tundra flag, because it was tundra colours: rust-red, reedy-brown and willow-green. Immediately after that house, the track ended abruptly with a hand-painted sign blocking the way. CAUTION DANGER, it read, because the road was gone. There was nothing but a two-metre drop down to the fast-flowing water.

Unless the air was still and the bugs awful, the CAUTION DANGER sign made a comfortable backrest for looking over the river. At high tide, the river was as wide as a city street, and on the far shore grew willow-scrub, then tundra to the horizon, all under the vastest sky. Sometimes it was silent by the river, but now that the salmon season was getting under way, metal skiffs passed at speed, driven by lads in waterproof overalls. If they saw me, I'd get the friendly, reticent wave.

On site, the workdays were long, but the evenings were free, and light until very late. After dinner one night Melia came with me to the CAUTION DANGER sign and identified the new birds I was seeing, the waders called yellowlegs, poking in the mud when the tide was out, warblers, and some familiars: snipe under the reeds, and flocks of teal. From time to time a merlin perched on a bare branch lodged in the river mud.

Curious, the owner of the last house joined us, a black-haired woman in a T-shirt and sweatpants, smoking a cigarette. She looked appraisingly at the swept-away road and said, 'They're moving my house soon. The land is eroding so fast. I come out here in the morning in my robe with a coffee, but every time more is gone. The next full moon tides, I think all this chunk of earth we're standing on will be gone.'

'Moving your whole house?'

'Yeah. All the houses down here. I don't want to move. I like this spot, the views. You can come here, catch a fish, even a seal. You can catch a goose for dinner...'

'Where will you be going?'

'Just up to the junction...' She pointed toward where a derelict cannery stood at the end of the road. 'It's not a nice view.'

* * *

Often in the evenings, a few villagers would come to the red building to see what had been discovered on the site. They were shy to enter, even though it was their own building, their own culture, their own site and stories.

There was always something new to show a visitor. In fact, every evening after dinner Rick conducted a popular little ritual called 'Artefact of the Day,' when the day's best finds were handed round to be admired. There was a good-natured vote for the 'best,' which

brought credit to its finder. It might be a line-weight shaped like a seal, or a pendant carved of mammoth ivory, or a piece of a basket made of woven grass, all preserved because frozen these five hundred years.

I grew to like the atmosphere in the village in the evening; the long gloamings before the sun set in ruby streaks behind the church. There was always the grind of four-wheelers but also the sounds of children laughing and playing, the thump of a basketball. Down at the river, all secret creeks and muddy inlets, rickety wooden fish-drying racks awaited their catch, and fishermen attended to their boats. Once, we met a young couple coming home from the tundra. The man was carrying a plastic tub brimful of berries, the woman had a puppy in her arms.

'Good picking!' said Melia. 'What'll you do with them?'

The girl spoke shyly. 'Make *akutaq*. Eskimo ice cream. You mix them with fat...'

'Seal fat?'

She pulled a face. 'No, something we buy from the store.'

The young man said. 'Back in the days when people lived in sod houses, they mixed the berries with caribou fat. We'll bring you some, yeah.'

* * *

July soon turned to August. One afternoon dozens of dragonflies with spotted wings hatched all at once from the damp mud around the site. The tide was far out, leaving only pools and reflections; phantasms shimmered on the horizon. A buxom elder arrived, driven by a youth on a four-wheeler along the beach. I half overheard the conversation: Rick and the elder were discussing Yup'ik names, which have meaning, but she was saying that the young people feel obliged to change them if they go away to college. I'd yet to hear a Yup'ik name.

Of the finds on the site, she said, every family had their own designs. She said, 'My ancestors tattooed their faces.'

Rick had said it's a matriarchal culture. If you need permission to do something, the ultimate decisions rest with women. Like the excavation, for example. It was the women elders who eventually gave permission.

'How do you find these women?' I asked.

'Oh, you find them. You'll be led there.'

That afternoon grew hot, over seventy degrees. In years past, the site couldn't open until the ground thawed in August, but that thaw was now occurring in July.

As the berry season began drawing to a close, so the salmon season opened and suddenly the whole town was talking about fish. From the screens we could count a dozen boats out at sea, especially on an incoming tide. They caught the salmon in nets as they were heading upriver to spawn. That was 'commercial fishing,' with the catches sold. There was also 'sports fishing,' when anglers from the southern USA came to spend time and money here, camping upriver with local outfitters. And then there was 'subsistence fishing,' with families catching enough to last them the winter. The fish would be frozen, or dried or smoked. Big salmon, the length of your arm.

One fisherman brought a gift of sixteen salmon to the red building. What to do? Cheryl the cook put the fish in buckets and asked the grocery store to keep them in their chill cabinets. She was planning a 'subsistence supper.' A dish of *akutaq* also appeared, perhaps from the young couple with the puppy. It didn't look promising, fat and berries mashed together, with a bit of green sourdock (the name just means 'mixture'), but it was dangerously good. High fat, high sugar, ideal for taking on long cold trips by dog-sled.

On the Wednesday, that week's *Delta Discovery* had arrived. The strapline said it was 'Alaska's largest independent Native-owned and operated newspaper.' It covered the whole delta, and its tone was couthy. The front page was devoted to a photo of two wee girls out on the tundra somewhere. *Iqvaryarluk!* Berry-picking! Inside was news of a 'burn closure,' which meant a ban on campfires and such, because the tundra was so dry and combustible. Warren, passing by, pointed over my shoulder to the article, saying, 'That's never happened before, round here.'

A cheery column called 'Chasing the Ambulance' listed the week's call-outs, in the notorious town of Bethel, from where the planes flew:

Medics responded to a report of an intoxicated person unable to walk. Upon arrival, the person was found sitting on the ground. Patient was assessed and taken to hospital.

A person who was suicidal.
A person bleeding from the head.
A bicycle accident.
An unconscious person in front of the United
  Pentecostal Church.

* * *

There was one elder who was particularly interested in the dig. The name he used was John Smith and he was the grandfather of Mike Smith. John was a youthful sixty-eight or seventy, small of stature. Like most of the men, he usually wore thick-checked lumberjack shirts and workmen's jeans. His greying hair was loosely slicked back. He had high cheekbones and a slightly flirtatious air with women. I suspect in his youth he may have had a bit of a quiff. He liked Johnny Cash.

He'd often drop by of an evening to see the day's finds, especially any pieces in walrus ivory, because he himself was a carver.

John was valued for his presence, his link to the Yup'ik language, his stories. He spoke slowly, as if weighing every word, but that seemed to be the Yup'ik way. Think first, speak slowly. He spoke also with his hands: gesturing, sometimes mimicking. He could mimic a bird with his hands.

One day, the excitement was an earring that had been found on site, carved of walrus ivory. It was a flat platelet, about one centimetre square, with two smaller pendant circles, a bit like owl eyes. The platelet itself had been carved with a dot amid concentric circles, which Rick said was a common design and may represent the all-seeing eye.

John took the earring into his hand, turned it, scrutinising it.

'How old is this?' he asked

'Five hundred years.'

'How'd they do that, without metal? Make those perfect circles?' He looked around at us, and said with reverence, 'What kind of people *were* they?'

'Your kind of people, John!'

We'd often hear John make remarks of wonderment and of sadness for the culture which was past.

'There are no Eskimos any more,' he'd say. 'All gone.'

John could remember sealskin-covered kayaks on the river. 'All gone now.'

And dog teams, and dog-sleds.

'Now, everyone uses outboard engines and snow-machines. Too. Much. Noise!'

'Do you know how to travel by dog-sled?' we asked.

'Yeah, I know.' He nodded, paused. 'You need seven dogs. *Smart* ones. They will find their own way home.'

He made a motion with his hands, exactly like the paws of a running dog.

'They smell their own trail.'

Then he re-enacted the feeding of sled dogs, one by one, throwing them a lump of blubber each.

When John told a story or an anecdote, or fetched something out of his memory, I had to listen closely. His voice was soft and often I was unsure whether the event happened to him, or his grandfather, or someone else entirely. I don't know whether it matters. It was a case of listening, and learning. For example, who was the man caught in an obliterating snowstorm when he was trying to reach home on his dog-sled? He had been travelling a long time and the blizzard was dreadful, but all at once the dogs stopped and refused to go on. Nothing would make the dogs move. So the man had to dig in and wait till the storm passed or the light came – and when it did, he realised the dogs wouldn't go home because they already were home. His house was right there.

Rick is only a few years younger than John.

'Huh,' Rick said ruefully. 'When he was out on a dog-sled, I was sittin' on a sofa watchin' TV.'

John came by every few evenings, and when he'd had enough he'd slip away again, but not before he'd made a little drawing if required. If one of the students had found an earring or a pendant, what better souvenir could she have of her time excavating a Yup'ik village than a replica made by a craftsman? Legally, only Native carvers are allowed to work in walrus ivory, and here was one right here, with his blue check shirt and jeans, and slow smile.

'The ivory – you have to work it with your hands. Ivory will become like soap. I learned from my uncle. I watched my uncle, sanded for him, polished. I listened to his stories. You have to be in a very quiet place.' He laughed. 'No kids!'

He kept a little workshop by his house near the river.

'John,' the girls would say. 'Can you make this, please?'

Enjoying the attention, he'd study the piece in question, turn it, feel it, then tilt his head. 'I can try.'

He'd ask a fair price. When he came back three or four days later, everyone would crowd round to see the finished work: pendants shaped like tiny seals, earrings with concentric circles. Designs that had lain in the earth for five hundred years were alive again, warming against the skin.

One evening I asked him a daft question. 'John,' I said. 'Where does your walrus ivory come from?'

'From a walrus!'

'Funny guy.'

'They come down here in spring, March time. On the ice.'

'I'd love to see a walrus.'

'Once, one swam upriver here. Taking shortcut to Hooper Bay. A teacher shot it with only a .22 magnum. We harpooned it and dragged it to an old couple at spring camp.'

The thought of a teacher shooting a walrus confounded me.

'Yeah,' said John, under the strip lights, 'We harpoon them. We gotta *remember*. If the planes stop flying and no food comes in, we gotta *remember* how to live.'

John mentioned that his wife was going berry-picking to a place she favoured somewhere upriver.

'Can we help?' asked Melia. 'Go with her? I love picking berries.'

John demurred, then gave his slow reply. 'She likes to be alone, on the tundra.'

'Not scared of bears?' I asked.

He gave me a smile. 'She talks to them.'

'What does she say?'

'She says: "I'm here. I'm here. *Quan-tah*. If you give them your presence, they'll leave you alone."'

Around that time there was a remarkable find. An undamaged *ulu* was recovered. An *ulu* is a woman's knife, with the blade set under the handle, and this one had a blade of greenish stone, still with a sharp edge. This handle was about five inches long, a nice fit in the palm. It was another woman who found it, one who happened to be an expert on such knives.

'Look,' Teresa said, as it was passed round. 'The handle's carved in the shape of a seal.' It had the swell of a seal's body and, when you looked at it front on, a seal's face looked back at you, dolefully, as though the seal knew exactly what the woman was about to do with her *ulu*, her knife.

When John Smith next came to the red building, he also turned the *ulu* in his hands, nodding in sad recognition. But at once he spotted something we had all missed. Yes, a seal. But look: if the seal is facing right, then what is facing left? A beluga whale! There's its eye, there's the blowhole, see?

Again he said, softly, 'We gotta remember. We tell the kids, you gotta remember! If the planes stop flying...'

After three or four days of freakish heat the weather cooled, the wind shifted, with an edge already hinting at autumn. Then came a morning of haar – cold sea fog. No planes flew. There was a sense of closing down.

When the others had gone to the site, five of us remained in the red building, where the conversation turned to language. We sat at the table in the windowless room, speaking in English. John Smith was there, and Erika Larsen, a photographer of Sami descent who had arrived on assignment from *National Geographic*. Also, an archaeologist from the Aleutian Islands, Sven Hakansson, an old colleague of Rick's and himself a Native American. The talk was about Native people being discouraged or even forbidden to speak their own languages: the language of memory, of materials, of the land, of the hands' work. Of having parents who'd become ashamed of 'that dirty language.' Of being sent to boarding school, where every day began with a chant: 'English is my language.'

Erika told us she had been on a course in Norway to learn something of the Sami language. It was noteworthy, she said, that those people who were most angry learned least.

Later, after the fog had cleared, word reached us that a snowy owl had been seen out by the airstrip. One of the pilots had spotted it when he was coming in to land. Melia suggested we take a run out there to look for it.

Beside the gravel runway, one small building housed a waiting room and a back office. In the office we discovered a young woman whose job was to log the aircraft as they came and went, and to make phone calls if one was late. 'Did you see a snowy owl here?' Melia asked. 'The pilot says he saw one when he was landing.'

The girl smiled shyly. 'Yeah,' she said. 'It's mine.'

'It's yours?'

'Yeah. We raised it up. My husband caught it up the river. It was a chick and we raised it up. The kids loved it. Then we let it go, just a few days ago. I got pictures on my phone...'

She showed us pictures of a man with a grey owlet on his gauntleted arm, a video of two toddlers hunkered down laughing as the owlet hopped around and tried to hide under the struts of the house.

Melia whispered, 'It's not a snowy owl, it's a great horned. Poor thing's scared.'

'What did you feed it on?'

'Mice. We set traps for mice. Bits o' fish.'

'And now it's out here?'

'Yeah.'

'Does it recognise you?'

She laughed. 'No.'

At the edge of the runway there was an upholstered seat, big enough for two, that looked as though it might have come from a bus. We sat there and surveyed the land, the mountains, the sky. A single patch of snow was shining in the mountains. We saw a couple of jaegers sitting on tussocks. No owl. A dark dot appeared in the sky which looked like a plane coming in, but then transformed into a flock of geese, already heading south.

Back at the red building, two of the postgraduate students were sorting through trays of bird-bones with tweezers. They were bones from geese or cranes which had been cut prior to making small objects, maybe needles or awls.

Finding these bones, and the seal/whale *ulu*, suggested that a women's work area had been exposed at Nunallaq. High-status women, judging by the jewellery finds. Matriarchs. A woman's belt had also been discovered, decorated with caribou teeth. John said, 'My aunt had a belt like that! It was her weapon. If you saw her untying that belt, you ran!'

I liked that people talked so readily and unembarrassedly about animals and birds and the land. They didn't give 'information,' instead they told incidents, anecdotes. Like coming at a subject sideways, not straight on. One morning I was standing by the grocery store looking out at the mountains, when a man joined me. I knew him only as George. He'd be in his sixties, with an earnest, attractive face. I knew him to see because he was the unassuming janitor who looked after the red building and the bunkhouse where we slept.

He had a mop in his hand.

'Whatcha looking at?' he said.

'The mountains.'

'When I was little, I used to go with my folks right there.' He pointed to a notch in the faraway hills. 'We hunted ground squirrels, April into May. Ground squirrels, you know? For making parkas, the fur at the bottom? Lots of ground squirrels there.'

'What else?'

'Old gold mines. All along there. My pa used to haul water for them. Fifty cents an hour.'

'Caribou?'

'All over. One time a caribou walked right here, into town. We all made a circle round it and caught it.'

We stood companionably for a moment or two more, then, 'Right.' He said. 'I gotta mop out the shower.'

I noticed that people notice. George had noticed me looking. They notice the bog cotton and its passing, an influx of owls, that there are bears around. The whole place must be in constant conversation with itself, holding knowledge collectively. One morning as I passed a wee boy on his way to school, he pointed to the sky and said 'Ducks!' Which there were, two of them, flying high.

No doubt they noticed us too, Melia and me with our binoculars, wandering round town.

On the beach halfway between the village and site lay the remains of a large sea mammal, long dead, just a big scapula and some leathery skin half buried in the dark sand. Not that I walked the beach, we'd been warned against it, and in truth it unnerved me with its silence and the cascading light, and the way the sea vanished to the horizon at low tide, leaving only sheeny pools.

But sometimes we got hold of a four-wheeler. Melia drove.

One day I asked Mike, 'Do you know what that dead animal is, down the beach near the creek? Is it a walrus?'

I wanted it to be a walrus.

'No, it's a bearded seal.'

The point was, I knew I'd get an answer, and it wouldn't be: 'What animal? I don't know. Can't say I'd noticed.'

The sub-Arctic summer was fleeting. The village felt busy, with berry-picking and fishing excursions. The school was now closed, but every day more flocks of geese passed over. Soon the show and tell would be held, the site covered over and backfilled for winter.

But – an invitation arrived. There was to be a birthday party and we were invited: Melia, myself, Erika the photographer, and her assistant, Val.

That evening, the four of us picked our way past sheds and smokehouses, bikes and garbage to reach a particular house. We took two of the sixteen salmon as a gift.

Duckboards had been laid down over the black water that oozed between the houses. You could understand the longing for the winter freeze and all-covering snow.

Our hostess was called Sarah and she was waiting to greet us at the top of the wooden stairs to her front door. Sarah was in her forties. Her younger sister Misty was there too, ready to usher us in. Like everyone else in town, they wore plain shop-bought sweatpants, hoodies, T-shirts. I recognised these two women because they had arrived at the site the day before and been shown round. I'd spoken to them myself in the finds tent.

There were introductions. We filed in, shaking hands with Misty and Sarah. We each gave our names. As we did so, Sarah looked at us from head to foot appraisingly, and then bestowed on each of us a Yup'ik name several syllables long. It seemed to delight her, matching us to these names by I don't know what qualities.

I understood that these names, which we now bore as well as our own, were the names of family members who had died. So it was as revenants, rather than strangers, that we were welcomed into Sarah's home. She had a calm presence, a similar quiet, think-about-it-first manner to John Smith, as many of the people here.

We were shown through a vestibule crowded with overclothes and boots, and into a living area no bigger than a static caravan, with a kitchen/diner on the left and on the right a living space with a wood stove and sofas round a coffee table, where elders and toddlers were disposing of a large, pink-iced birthday cake. A pink banner read 'Birthday Princess.' The birthday girl was only two.

Every shelf and dresser was crammed with the goods of a working family; a family of fisherfolk and hunters. It was Nunallaq in its modern manifestation.

At table we were offered a seafood salad with salmon roe, then *akutaq*, with salmonberries and sourdock, which was fresh and excellent. Also jelly and doughnuts and tea in pretty cups. The *akutaq* initiated a conversation about berries and berry-picking, about excursions out on to the tundra of two or three days at a time. Any conversation about food – and these folk speak a lot about food – becomes a conversation about the land or the sea. The salmonberry was best of all, queen of the berries, but, as we knew, their season was passing now, and the fishing season well under way.

Visitors or family members came and went, just saying hello, lads in their workgear, round-faced wrinkled elders wearing anoraks. The family spoke between themselves in Yup'ik. The toddler was fussed over until she was tired.

When one particular elder arrived, I think the sisters' mother, and we rose to greet her, Sarah introduced us by the Yup'ik names we were carrying. The invocation of these lost people affected the old lady and she hugged us all warmly one by one.

After a while, after the elders and toddlers had quietly disappeared, another woman arrived, an elder sister to Sarah and Misty. Her name was Grace. She had a similar oval face to Sarah, a similar calm manner. She had brought something wrapped in a blue towel which she wanted us to see. The table was cleared and the towel unfolded. Before us lay stone arrowheads, net weights, hammer stones, lithics which Grace had found over the years, on the beach, washed out from the land.

We picked them up, tested their edges. Grace said she took the collection to the school from time to time to discuss with the children.

I asked, 'But you haven't been to the site, to see the excavation?'

Grace shook her head quickly.

'You've really never been? You should come, really – it would interest you so much. Misty and Sarah came yesterday...'

She shook her head again, emphatically. It was odd.

As with the names, I didn't want to press for explanations. But then Grace said, 'I found a mask once and brought it home. But I heard laughing. A woman. Like a shaman. A nasty laughing. So I took it right back where I'd found it.'

The talk turned back to fish and fishing, an easier topic, and ocean currents, and encounters with marine creatures. Misty spoke about dolphins, and of a moment once near Kodiak when two bow-headed whales had come rising out of the deep, flanking their boat.

Conversation was easy and we sat up late. The gloaming light lingered at the window, pinking and reddening as the evening passed. At almost midnight, when the northern horizon was a chalky amber, Sarah led us outside and down the steps and along the duckboards to her smokehouse. We stooped and entered. The shed smelled deliciously and anciently of woodsmoke. Strips of salmon hung from the low rafters. She cut some for us and we hunkered down to eat yet more food – strips of chewy smoked salmon.

When we emerged, the sky was the same deep red as the fish, and silhouetted at the creek were the rackety fish-drying houses, now filling with the year's catch.

'Don't bears come, and take the fish when they're drying? It looks like an open invitation,' I asked.

'We have people out on bear-watch.'

'All night?'

'Yes. My son is out there now. They watch up at the airstrip – that's the way the bears come. Or down the other side of the river.'

'And if they saw a bear, would they shoot it?'

Sarah shrugged mildly. 'Shoot the guns, scare it away.'

It was a jewel of a night, I didn't want to go to my windowless bunkroom, so waited up till the stars shone in an ink-blue sky. I was glad to have been welcomed into a home, a warm clutter. I recognised much. Sarah's cabin was as cramped as a two-room tenement. I recalled my own long-dead grandmothers, both called Margaret, whose names I also carry, and their homes I loved as a child.

Small cramped houses.

Next evening one of the village lads turned up in the red building with a big bandage round his hand.

'What did you do?'

'Punched a sign.'

'And – why did you punch a sign?'

'Uh,' he said. 'Family issues.'

* * *

The site attracted photographers and journalists. A radio reporter arrived on the plane. She was from the south, but now lived in Bethel, a predominantly Yup'ik town.

'Is it as bad as people say?' I asked her, when no one else could hear.

'Well,' she said. 'It's got a lot of nicknames. Beth-hell, they call it. As you know it's the regional hub, it's got lots of problems. Alcohol. Heroin is there now. Domestic abuse. Suicides. The churches – they were the agents of colonisation – they're all there.

'We've had nine suicides in the region this year. They're killing themselves and each other. STDs are the highest level in the state. Teenage pregnancy. It's a huge mess. But the culture, the stories...

'The big row now is whether to open a liquor store.

You get these white people – they turn up, they're all libertarian. "Hell, why should I have my baggage searched for booze?" But we're guests, the way I see it. We should do what the Yup'ik people decide.

'It needs strong leadership, but the leadership structures are those the colonists imposed, so they just replicate themselves and the Native leaders become self-serving.

'My partner and I want children,' she said, 'but we wouldn't do that there.'

* * *

A day or so later I was helping on the screens, shoving mud back and forth with a trowel. Out at sea, a dozen small, one-man fishing boats worked at the nets. Inland, a lone cloud was drifting over the tundra, as though looking for somewhere to rain.

The day's earth was heavy and damp. Mike Smith arrived with a bucketful.

'We're becoming experts on dirt.'

'That's what archaeology is!' he said.

I asked Mike how he became involved with the dig. He grinned. This was a story he likes to tell.

'Well. I was sixteen, you know. Teenager. I was in a bad way. Didn't want to see anyone, didn't see any point in anything.

'So I went off down the beach on my own. And down here, you know, I saw four or five white guys, sort of digging. I thought: Uh, just crazy white guys.

'But I was curious. So I went back up and that's how I met Rick. Before I knew it I was on the screen, like this, and I found a dart. Well that was that, I was hooked. And you know I'm down here as often as I can be. It's given me...' He didn't finish the sentence.

'Don't you fancy going off to college?'

'No, I'm a village boy. I don't do too well out of the village. I've been to the Lower 48 on a school trip but I got homesick.'

'Well,' I said, 'it takes brains to run a village.'

'Yeah, a village boy. I'd just like a house here, and to go fishing. Maybe run a trap-line.'

A smell was rising from the earth in the screen. It was familiar, domestic, not unpleasant. I worked on, wondering if I was imagining it, because it was the smell of cooking. Specifically, the smell of mince and tatties, staple dish of my childhood.

'Mike – I'm hallucinating. Can you smell that?'

'The meaty smell? It's because we're down at the house floor now, where they did the processing. Seals, walrus meat, skinning, all that.'

The air is so clean and sharp, you can smell seal-meat from five hundred years ago.

We worked on. Below us, the daily routines and rhythms of the site. There were harriers around and ravens. Small wonder, if the smell of ancient meat was wafting over the land. I stopped to watch a harrier lift and tilt head down over the dunes, barely moving its wings as it hunted. Following the harrier were three ravens. Not only following, they seemed to be mimicking, even mocking, it. As it moved, they moved. Three ravens teasing a harrier.

* * *

Cheryl the cook produced her 'subsistence supper' and it was a triumph. She made a broth of barley and musk-ox meat, then a chilli dish of moose meat. Melia, devotee of fish, grilled two different species of salmon on a gas barbecue outdoors.

Mike stayed in the red building for dinner. He'd brought from home a wolverine pelt to show us. Thick and hardish guard hairs, coffee-coloured, very serious claws.

'Are there wolverines in the mountains?'

'Way far.'

'Did you tell us you wanted to run your own trap-line?'

'But I wouldn't want to trap wolverine. They're too dangerous. Their bite is lethal. A wolverine can kill a bear!'

Over dinner Mike talked us through the Yup'ik culinary year, which is to say the year on the land and sea and river. It is a tight timetable. Right now, as we knew, was the end of berry-picking: salmonberries, blueberries, they were almost done. It had been a good berry year, the women were happy. Now salmon fishing was well under way. The town was half empty; the river busy with roaring boats. A net strung at the rivermouth could yield sixty fish in an hour.

Upriver, it was line fishing. The fish must be caught, prepared, dried, frozen, smoked before the winter ahead.

After the salmon comes the moose-hunting season. Then trout. Then comes a settling down for winter, always with the hope of good deep proper snow and ice, like they used to get, because ice and snow mean you can travel quickly over the tundra, or up the frozen river to seek the caribou that come down from the hills with their attendant wolves. Upriver, you can collect firewood. You can visit other villages.

Winter also means ptarmigan, for ptarmigan soup, which is best served, Mike said, with a drizzle of seal oil. Spring ice means ice-fishing for walrus and seals.

Young Mike, in his calf-length shorts, his black hoodie and shades, told us now about seal-hunting. 'I did my first sealhunt this winter. Me and my brother. But he's too trigger happy.' You shoot with your rifle first, and having shot the animal you get a tiny chance before it dives to throw your harpoon. The harpoon is fitted with a float so it doesn't sink too. You know you've hit the seal because of the smell, you can smell seal oil heated by the bullet.

At table, he was enjoying a small, attentive audience, poised over our moose meat and fish.

'I snare snowshoe hares too,' he said. 'Hare soup served with seal fat! You cook it up, mix in a little seal fat ... mmmm. I give the skins away to people who make mittens. But you gotta be quick before the fox gets the hare. Often I've gone back to the snare to find just a mess of blood and fur.'

Mike prefers walrus skin to the meat. Especially delicious is walrus skin with the fat still attached. He held up finger and thumb to show the depth of fat under a walrus's skin – about three inches. 'Mmm-mmm, I like that.'

'Mike,' we said, 'you should open a Yup'ik restaurant! In Paris or New York. It would cause a sensation. Walrus skin with a jus of seal oil.'

'Then, when the pools thaw on the tundra, women collect pond-greens. They have to dig 'em up with a stick before they flower. And birds' eggs. I got seagulls' eggs up at the airstrip. I think that seagull knows me now. It swoops at me.'

Our own dessert was fresh tundra berries with ice cream. Mike pushed his chair back to be first in line.

'Hey,' we teased him, 'what happened to the walrus blubber and seal oil?'

He grinned. 'Man, I *like* ice cream.'

* * *

There was a particular place on the tundra near the site where Melia wanted to spend a little time bird-watching, so we went there one bright afternoon. She led and I followed.

We were less than half a mile from the track but the tundra encircled us, under its dome of sky. We walked on a low bright carpet of berry-plants and mosses. Suddenly a young short-eared owl flew up right in front of us. It had sat tight till it could bear it no longer; we were close enough to hear the papery shiver of its wings as it lifted away, hopefully to resettle somewhere nearby where its parent would find it.

On a long tussock we set up the telescope. Here, we were visible, giving our presence to bears, as John had said. On the tussock grew dwarf birch, a few salmonberries with leaves turning red, and Labrador tea. The difference in altitude of only a few inches supported a different fauna to the lower land around. Between us and the mountains grew miles of shifting, breathing greens; damp-loving grasses that fringed invisible ponds and waterways.

We chose to sit quietly, and in a short space of time, maybe twenty minutes of looking out over the landscape, I realised my eyes were adjusting, my vision sharpening.

There was the close-at-hand, flowers and bright berries where we sat, then the middle distance, which resolved itself into bands of different grasses, each swaying in the breeze in its own way. In the far distance, a heat haze shimmered from the land. Black wavering shapes were ravens rising and falling through the air.

We looked at the land, and at a pond where Melia had noticed a number of different ducks and waterfowl; it was these she wanted to watch. Grebes and shovellers with little parties of chicks setting sail across the blue water. Sometimes, a rare and beautiful Aleutian tern flew in. I was happy just to sit quietly in the company of someone who also enjoyed spells of quietude.

After thirty minutes or so, I could see colours better, until the haze distorted them. Details emerged. How had I failed to notice the three grass stems next to my right knee, bound together by a ball of spiderweb? When a pale bee entered a fireweed flower, it was an event.

A quiet meditation. Melia sat some yards away, half turned to look southward, occasionally lifting her binoculars, naming a bird she saw. My hearing sharpened too: after forty-five minutes I could distinguish the different sounds the breeze made in the various grasses. A little bird nearby was making a buzzing noise, like a small electrical fault. The ripple of pondside reeds, the light on distant mountains. Then an owl appeared, labouring toward us with a fat lemming drooping from its claws. It landed silently fifty yards away, watching us. We hoped it was feeding the young one we'd disturbed. Its cat-like owl eyes stared at us through the long grass-stems.

We watched the tundra, but the tundra, they say, is watchful too. The people say, 'It's like something's looking at you.'

There are stories of disappearance and reappearance, out on the tundra.

Was it John who told the story of the two men out on the tundra in fog? The fog was so low, just above their heads. But a hole appeared in the fog and from the hole they could hear laughter and merriment. 'Give me a leg up,' said one of the men. 'I want to see what's happening.' 'Okay, but you must reach for me in turn, and pull me up too,' said the other. So the first man entered the world above the cloud, but at that moment the hole closed and the bank of fog moved on, and the first man was never seen again.

The story of another man, who got lost on the tundra and was given up, but who walked back into the village years later, wearing the very same clothes.

The story of the little spirit woman appearing to a lost hunter, with a drum, dancing to the beat of her drum. She was on a hillock. 'But I knew I mustn't follow her, I knew I mustn't...'

The story of the rain-cloud. The woman was out collecting berries and had stayed too long, become a bit exposed and sunstroked. 'But,' she said, 'a little cloud came, right above my head and let down rain, it filled the leaves with rain for me to drink. How grateful I was to that cloud!'

After an hour, my senses were still clarifying. Perhaps it would never stop.

Now a loon was passing overhead, against the bright clouds, with a long thin fish trailing from its beak.

Then Melia saw cranes. She called my attention and together we watched seven or eight sandhill cranes flying in, low and slow, then land one by one, and begin to stalk through the grasses on long legs.

By then the grasses were so vibrant I could almost taste them. This, after only an hour of attention. What would a year be like, a lifetime, a thousand years? How attuned a person, a whole people, could become.

Who can say which story is 'true' and which not, when the tellers' senses are so acute? Rick says of the Nunallaq site that, if the inhabitants could come back now, walking over the tundra with their parkas and berry baskets, their piercings and tattoos, they would recognise their landscape. It hasn't changed that much.

'What would they have seen, back then, coming home?' I asked.

'Grass-roofed houses, fish-drying racks, dogs. Not so different, maybe, as now.'

John Smith was on good form when we saw him later, in the red building.

'We saw cranes!' Melia said, whereupon he stretched his arms and hunched his shoulders in imitation of the cranes' long-winged flight, his hands flapping slightly.

'They come close and swoop over you,' he said. 'Have you seen them dance? They're the first ones to lay eggs.'

'Do you eat cranes?'

That slow wide-eyed nod. 'We put everything in there – spice, stuffing.'

Now, with his hands and eyes, John became an owl. 'This year there's a lot of owls.'

* * *

A couple of days after the birthday party, I left the red building after dinner intending to take a walk. It was another beautiful, calm evening, impossible to spend it all indoors under the strip lights.

Outside, half a dozen kids had climbed the roof of a derelict-looking shed and were sliding down, dropping to the ground below then running round to climb again. I say derelict-looking, but that's lazy. I was learning to read the village better. Some sheds were fishermen's stores. Some small ones were smokehouses, where salmon was smoked. Wooden ones with a vestibule and a small chimney and a heap of dry driftwood, they were *maqiqs*:

steam baths. Saunas. A couple of times a week someone would come to the red building and say they were firing up the *maqiq* and they had space for a couple more. Two or three tired and dirty students would go, according to gender, and arrive back very red and very clean.

I turned left, but didn't get far before Sarah drew up on a four-wheeler. It pleased me that there were people in town I could recognise and name.

'Where are you going?' she asked.

'Nowhere. Just a walk.'

'Want to come for a ride?'

It wasn't a Harley, but why not? I clambered up onto the luggage rack beside her and held on as she drove the track down to the creek.

It was low tide, the water shone gold in the setting sun. Drawn up at the bank were a dozen metal skiffs, while out in the stream a man was using his own four-wheeler to nudge a boat to shore.

'That's my niece's husband,' said Sarah. She watched him for a few moments, then seemed satisfied, so turned and headed back up to town.

'Are you going somewhere in particular?' I asked.

'No. The house was too ... I wanted to come out.'

'I know what you mean.'

Next we rode on down the road toward the derelict cannery. 'That's the old graveyard,' said Sarah, as we passed a place I'd walked by often. There was nothing to mark it as a graveyard except knowledge, memory. We passed the cannery, then continued down the three-quarter mile to the beach, rocking down the dunes onto the sand. Sarah turned right toward the rivermouth, then stopped again to watch the few boats still out fishing.

The low sun blazed, we blocked it with our hands, the sea was liquid fire. We watched a boat manoeuvring. It was looking, Sarah said, for the channel into the river. 'He's found it.'

Again she seemed satisfied, turned the four-wheeler on the sand and asked, 'Where do you want to go?'

'Anywhere you like, Sarah. It's nice to be cruising around.'

We rocked back along the beach. It was as if she had come out purely to notice things, check all was well. Care-taking.

We left the beach again, back over the sand dunes.

'This rye grass, we use it for making baskets. My sister you met, she makes baskets. Her husband is an ivory carver.'

After a few hundred yards, Sarah halted the vehicle again. This meant she had something to tell me. Sometimes she paused, the think-before-you-speak manner. Notice things, speak with forethought. She pointed toward the wind turbines and communications mast.

'You see the fence next to the lagoon? Last September, I think it was September, my nephew was driving out past there, and he saw something. *Something* stood up real slow, and that fence only came up to its chest.'

'What was it?'

'A Hairy Man! Another time my sister's family was up at the old airport...'

Then her cell phone rang and she fetched the phone out from the pocket of her grey hoodie and took the call.

'I gotta go back.'

We drove into town. Dogs were running around in the dust. Children played. In the north-west, the sun was hidden behind bands of purple, fire-rimmed cloud.

* * *

Sunday came, and Melia had news. With the salmon running, Warren and his family were going upriver in their boat. They'd be fishing. We could join them. We might even reach the mountains. We could help with the cost of fuel. We'd get a trip, they'd get fish. We'd all be out of the village.

We were a party of six: Melia and me, Warren, his teenage son Patrick, his wife Jeanette and Teddi, Jeanette's sister. I recognised Teddi from the grocery store, where she was manager. Teddi was the one who ordered in all the goods. Both women were petite, dark-haired and quietly competent. They tied their black hair back and wore combat trousers, hoodies and ball caps.

To reach the boats we borrowed the yellow station wagon and drove about a mile and a half to where the road ended at a series of gravel pits. Hauled up every tidal creek were grey, flat-bottomed metal skiffs: every family seemed to possess at least one. But they're small, so we split ourselves between two boats. Warren manned the first, standing next to the hefty outboard engine; young Patrick drove the other. Of course, they took fishing rods. Of course, they took a powerful rifle, tucked away in the stern.

Out on the quick river, Warren and Patrick's skill lay in putting their boats into the right channel, the best braid, in judging speed and cornering against the onrush as the river widened and narrowed.

Hazards included half-submerged logs that had been swept down from forests in the distant interior, and the way the river looped right, then left. It was exhilarating to be out of town, to be moving at speed. Every fleet-flowing bend was paired with a reef of grey shingle. Gulls flew up from these reefs as we neared.

I sat in the front, trying to be vigilant, hoping to see bear or moose or birds on the riverbanks, but the engines were loud. Warren wore shades and ear protectors; it was too loud to speak.

Because it was salmon season we passed camps at the riverside and many fishermen standing on the gravel banks. These were big bearded men from the southern states. The Quinhagak Corporation owns the land and rivers, they provided the services, stores, boats and camps, and took the fees. The clients took the fish. That was the deal. Solemnly, the fishermen waved as we zipped by. They were surprised, I think, not at the dark-haired Yup'ik women in the boats – they scoot upriver all the time, berry-picking or hunting – but at the white women in their company. The fishing trips looked to be all male.

After some miles of headwind and river spray with the mountains growing nearer, Warren and Patrick slowed the boats and nudged them against one of the

shingle beaches. They could resist no longer: they had
to catch fish. Teddi and Jeanette secured the boats with
ropes and they all wasted no time in assembling their
fishing rods. I wandered off a few yards, stepping over
a bear pat, brown and crusty. It was the diameter of a
saucer and decorated with undigested red berries. A
paw print not much smaller was pressed into the silt
nearby.

'Did you smell that bear back there?' asked Warren.

I'd seen him wrinkle his nose and point to the bushes
of the riverbank, but hadn't understood.

Thinking the fishing would take ages, I hunkered on
a washed-up log to wait. I looked at the grey shingle at
my feet and a spray of yellow poppies in bloom among
the stones. I kept an eye out for bears among the willow
scrub on the bank opposite, and watched Teddi casting
her line out into the river. The air was not quite warm,
not quite cold. Dark clouds were gathering and a breeze
rising, the kind of breeze that precedes rain. I prepared
myself to be bored, but within ten minutes Teddi and
Warren had each landed a hefty coho salmon.

The fish were smacked hard on the head with a stick
and gutted at once, then stowed in a polythene bag.
Out in the water further salmon twisted, trout too, all
pushing and nudging up to their spawning grounds. I had
never seen so many fish.

With the salmon in the bag, we made to leave, but first
Jeanette shyly produced lollipops – a flat boiled-sweet
kind I hadn't seen in years. The women sucked lollies,
the men smoked cigarettes, and then we pushed the boats

out and jumped in. The riverbanks began to rise higher, and in a mile or two more trees appeared, cottonwoods, releasing a dreamy autumnal smell. From time to time we passed beaver lodges. Then we turned a leftward bend and slowed because there was a bald-eagle nest nearby, and sure enough an eagle took off at our approach. In a shallow we idled, watching as the bird made a wide loop overhead, and listening for Patrick's boat. It didn't come. We waited some minutes more. Jeanette told us the Yup'ik name for the eagle. Warren told us that cottonwood is favoured for making harpoons to hunt seals.

After a while, we turned back downstream to see what was up, and found the second boat pulled up on a shingle bank strewn with bleached driftwood. Engine trouble. This was the reason Warren had wanted to take two boats: just in case. The river felt like a highway, but like a highway, as soon as you stop and silence falls, you feel the scale of the vast land around, its pressing strangeness, your exposure. At least I did. We hadn't seen any other boats or fishermen for a while.

Washed up on this bank were plenty of sticks, so as Warren and Patrick concentrated on the engine Teddi and Jeanette set about making a windbreak. As with the fishing, they were quick of hand. First they gathered a few branches. They rammed these into the silt, wove more branches between and draped the frame with a blue plastic sheet. This we huddled under, because it was starting to rain. As they built a fire, I watched carefully. The sisters worked as a team, bent over with heads together, barely speaking because they didn't have to. First they scooped out some gravel to make a shallow pit about a foot long. They filled the pit with dry grasses they'd gathered at the shore, then laid thin twigs over in a lattice. On top of that came bigger sticks. One lick of flame from Teddi's Zippo lighter and the fire caught.

Within fifteen minutes the sisters had provided shelter and heat. Food they had secured already. I felt like I was seeing them in their element. Not the day job, but the river, the tundra. Now, they went scouting for fresh willow wands among the thickets behind the beach. As the fire gained heat they whittled the willow wands with knives until they were sharp. Then, from the boat they took not the fresh salmon but hot-dog sausages, and rammed them onto the sticks. Everyone hunkered, cooking hot dogs over the fire. I didn't want to ask about the salmon, maybe they were saving it, but Teddi read my mind, and smiled a calm smile. 'Hot dogs cook quickest!' she said.

Jeanette was listening to her iPod. I don't know what she was listening to, but I liked the way she travelled: with her iPod in one pocket and her *ulu* in the other.

Something vital had broken in the engine. We were too many, strictly speaking, for one boat, so it was decided that Patrick would wait alone on this bank, with the defunct boat, the fire and the gun. The rest of us would continue upriver for a while. We wouldn't reach the mountains, but we'd go see what we could see.

As we left Patrick sitting cross-legged by the fire, I asked him, 'Are you not scared?'

'Scared o' what?' he replied, mildly.

I shrugged. The size of the place. Loneliness. The cold, black clouds. Hungry bears.

'Done it before,' he said. 'All night.'

'Scared of what?' said his father. 'This is our backyard.'

* * *

I don't know how many miles we travelled, maybe thirty, because the river looped so much. In time, however, the riverbanks grew into soft hillocks, and thicker bushes crowded the banks. Then, at a place where the river split in two channels, Warren nudged the boat ashore at the north bank and anchored it with a metal plate thrust into the earth. We left the boat and scrambled up a bluff covered in low vegetation; we must have gained a little altitude because the leaves here were already crispy with autumn hints. When we'd climbed about two hundred feet above the water we reached a rounded summit. Bedrock was breaking through, the first rock I'd felt for weeks, and what I saw from that summit astonished me.

I was looking out at land. Land, every way one turned. From this small hill the tundra was laid out below like a green sea, sedgy and subtle and glinting with secret melt-pools and waterways. It was land relishing its brief summer, open and free to breathe. To west, south and north the land seemed unbounded, but inland there rose range after range of low, grey-blue mountains, the source of the river, with shadows in their glens and corries.

Above all, the sky. Every hue of sky was present at once, here a shower, there rays of sunshine filtering through, there openings of blue, and every white and grey of cloud. Shadows of clouds drifted over the land. It was a dream vision, a mythic view of land before farms, before towns and roads, unparcelled, unprivatised, whole.

We sat on the ground in the light breeze. Warren lit a Marlboro, Jeanette offered more lollipops. I sucked a red one, and could have looked out over that land forever. In a sense, Warren and Teddi and Jeanette have been. I wondered how their thoughts ran when they got out here, away from the village and the Corporation and all the social problems and well-intentioned schemes, and just looked at their land, land they had managed to retain.

Warren was squatting a few feet away, his camouflage jacket hunched over his shoulders. After a few minutes of silent looking, I ventured to speak.

'Warren. This is some backyard.'

He smoked on wordlessly, but then with his cigarette between his fingers he pointed southward over the intricate, mazy land, all sage green and emerald green and russet. He said, 'That's where I go wolf-hunting.'

Then he pointed east, over the plain spread before the mountains, and said, 'One time, 'bout five years ago, I came up here and all that place was covered in caribou...' He paused, carried on looking. Then: 'Our elders taught us to look for ravens. When a raven swoops, something is down there. If there's a bunch of them, they might be following a moose or a bear. If you suddenly hear seagulls, something's crossing the river.'

'How long have you people been here?'

''Bout ten thousand years. In winter we come up here on snow machines. Go over to Eek.'

The others reappeared over the brow of the hill. They'd been off scouting for bears but had had no luck. We wanted to spot a bear because Melia and I were going home soon, and there hasn't been a wild bear in Scotland for a thousand years. But there were no bears nearby. 'They'll be at the salmon spawning grounds on the side creeks,' Teddi said.

Then Warren told about hunting a bear. He spoke with no self-aggrandisement or swagger. On the contrary. He'd been young at the time and out hunting with his father. 'Shoot it!' said his father. He shot the bear. Twice. Then his father scored lines on the dead bear, in preparation for skinning it, and handed Warren the knife, saying, '*Your* bear, *your* responsibility.'

'It look me three days to skin that bear. I never hunted bear again.'

Too soon we had to leave, edging back down to the river in its channel and the waiting boat. Down there, the dream vision of the land was gone. I felt I'd had a glimpse of something – and a glimpse is all we have in this life.

Back at the shingle beach, Patrick had kept the fire burning. The rain had passed. Again the sisters set to work – now we would eat salmon. They took one of the morning's catch, wrapped it in tinfoil and set it in the hot embers. Then the fishing lines came out again, and as the first fish baked they landed several more. I could not believe the number of fish. When the fire-baked salmon was ready, we hunkered round the fire, eating its hot, pink flesh with our fingers. Then came a gateau Teddi had brought from the store; it was only slightly bashed. Having eaten, we travelled downstream again, bringing Patrick with us. They'd come back another day for the boat with the faulty engine. Right now we were going with the flow, swooping and turning with the Kanektok.

But we weren't done fishing. Some miles downstream we put into a slow, green easy backwater aside from the main channel. Here, in the waters around a grassy islet, there flashed the scarlet sides of sockeye salmon, dozens of them. Like silk slashes in a Tudor sleeve, the fish parted the water's surface as they moved. Again we left the boat, again the rods came out. It was appalling. Having spawned, the salmon were rotting even before they died. Red and stylish in the water, they emerged from it like things of nightmare, mouldering, hook-faced, blotched. They were so plentiful, all our hosts had to do was choose one, throw a hook at it and haul it in. One after another the fish were landed. They flapped listlessly on the mud, then were beaten over the head. Fifteen, twenty fish skulls broke with a wet smacking sound.

As Teddi had predicted, bears had been here, and perhaps still were, though we couldn't smell them. On the ground among the riverside shrubs were strewn the half-chewed bodies of a dozen fish. Such profligacy!

Having killed the fish, Teddi sliced off their heads with the curved blade of her *ulu*. When she threw the salmon heads back into the clear water, dozens of smaller fish shoaled round to investigate.

I wasn't going to get off without fishing, and soon enough Warren handed me his rod and line, and showed me how to hold it. I'd never fished before, so stood in the stern of the boat and inexpertly dangled the hook in the water. In two minutes a trout came, simple as that, like a magic creature in a folk tale, surrendering itself to me. I pulled and wound it in, the rod bending, the fish gleaming as it rose.

* * *

The vision of the land stayed with me. That night, in my dark bunk, I tried to imagine it by moonlight, the whole plain covered in caribou. In truth, it almost reminded me of Scotland. The ice-worn hills were almost like Highland Perthshire but on a vaster scale, and the colours brighter and light more intense, and there were no roads or towns, no pylons or farms or dams or big houses with rich private landowners.

There were fugitive creatures. Wolves and wolverines and bears. Rivers full of fish.

* * *

If you imagine all the incidents the people here spoke of, all the looking and listening, the stories and encounters, remembered and repeated and layered over thousands of years, you might indeed come to know your own backyard. And how it might help you. From two different sources I heard the story of the young man, some decades ago, who went with friends out onto the sea-ice. They'd been hunting, but he somehow got separated from the others, and when he tried to reach land and home he couldn't, because the ice had drifted away from the shore. Alone on the ice, he survived *for four months*. All he had was the clothes on his back, and his tools and weapons – and the knowledge his elders had bequeathed him.

We were told that story, and others, not in a sod hut lit by a seal-oil lamp, certainly not in an igloo, but in the red building – a metal-clad shed raised on stilts, harsh with electric strip lights. Does that matter? The stories came from people so softly spoken, and arrived so unexpectedly, and were over so soon, I wondered if I'd heard them at all.

The Yup'ik people might be spiritual, for want of a better word, but they're deeply practical, attuned to the land for good reason. The next day Warren was again striding toward his office, harassed as ever, cell phone pressed to his ear, but when he spotted me he came over to deliver a formal thank you.

'In our tradition,' he said, 'the first fish you catch you must give to an elder. I gave your trout to my mother. She sends her thanks. She says, "Now my belly is full."'

* * *

It was the last week of the dig, and there approached the finale which required days of preparation on the part of conservators like Melia: the annual 'show and

tell.' It would take place in the red building. All the best
artefacts would be laid out on display, with everyone in
town encouraged to come and see and talk about them.
A hot-dog stand would be erected outside, with salmon
broth for the more traditional-minded elders.

As well as Quinhagak folk, journalists and anthro-
pologists were flying in. Maybe a TV crew. Melia now
spent her days in the 'lab,' selecting the best of the
finds, cleaning them ready to be displayed, arranging
them according to theme. Posters went up at the school
and store, the coin-op laundry, the clinic and the post
office.

When I took a poster down to the tribal office, where
Mike Smith held a day job, there was another big poster
on the wall already. 'Birds on the Subsistence Harvest
Survey,' it said, and showed dozens of images of birds.
Each bird was depicted with its English name and a
blank box, for people to write in their local names.
Someone with a biro had written in the Yup'ik names:

Pacific loon: *Tunutillek*
Common loon: *Qaqatak*
Crane: *Qucillgak*

Jeanette was there and with her help I mastered, momen-
tarily, *Qucillgak* and *Qaqatak*, the crane and the loon.
Soft and irresisting sounds, like the tundra in summer, all
'qs' and 'ks' and 'ochs.'

'You sound like a Yuup!' said Mike.

'That'll be right!'

When the Thursday came round, the day of the 'show and tell,' those not out on site excavating until the last moment remained behind at the red building for a marathon of preparation.

Every horizontal surface was cleared of mugs, laptops, chargers, trays of fishbones, trays of woodchips, and then cleaned. The floor was scrubbed, furniture rearranged. When the hall was presentable, on its walls were hung photographs of the site: diggers huddled and grinning, Rick posing with a theodolite, Mike at a screen with the tundra receding into the distance.

The preparations could have been for a village wedding or a bring-and-buy sale. By 4 p.m. the tables were ready, the photos mounted, and all the selected artefacts, hundreds of them, were laid out according to theme, each in a little open plastic box, each resting on the carefully numbered bag to which it had to be returned. Melia worried that artefacts would become separated from their numbers, from their contexts. Like the people who made them, they were part of a community, a culture.

The students had scrubbed up nicely. Showers had been taken, clean shirts fetched from the bottom of backpacks. The hall began the day smelling of bleach, but soon the slow-cooking fish broth took over. It was a wintery atmosphere, despite the bright sunshine outside.

Then everything was ready. The students were stationed like stallholders, each with a water-spray to keep the artefacts slightly damp, especially the wooden ones.

It was like the anxiety before a party – will anyone come? At 4 p.m. I went to the door and was glad to see four-wheelers approaching down the street, people strolling over from their houses.

The first visitor was an elder in a turquoise headscarf with her adult grandson. They began at the beginning, heads bowed over a long table laid with arrowheads and hunting tools, harpoon parts. Then a school party arrived, with the headteacher. How many of these people I now knew by sight. With the children, the noise level increased. The schoolkids fastened on the table of gaming pieces. Dice made of bone, and darts. Then the array of dolls, so called, the flat sticks with three lines for a face, which may be simple toys, or maybe not.

There were the wooden masks and maskettes. A whole table was devoted to jewellery and adornment.

Then came household things: spoons of wood, knives of stone. Favourite pieces were like old friends: the whale/seal *ulu*, the bowl released from the ice, a wooden carving of an owl. The materials were driftwood, antler, bone, grass, ivory, stone. The materials were the gifts of other creatures: fish, owls, caribou, seals, walrus, whales.

The place was full of life. People wore jeans, hoodies, *kuspuks*; men came in their working clothes with high-vis jackets and boots. Small children were held up to view the objects. The students had to be vigilant, to make sure things weren't picked up and put down in the wrong place.

As the room filled and the sound of conversation grew, I wandered round table to table, eavesdropping.

'And you'd pull the bow like *this*...'

'A *lamp*! My mother had one.'

'Nowadays we use synthetic sinew, ballistic nylon.'

I saw George, the water man. The last time I'd spoken to him he had a mop in his hands. Here he was again, but he'd swapped the mop for his seal-hunting harpoon, which stood taller than he did. He was showing the students how his modern harpoon toggle compared to those of his Yup'ik forebears at Nunallaq. His was the same shape, same mechanism, but made of brass.

A lady came with a basket she had woven from beach grass. She was plump and wore a bright floral *kuspuk* and tracksuit bottoms. Her basket was bowl-shape, a foot deep and decorated with stylised flowers in what looked like strips torn from an old polythene bag, but no, she said, it's seal-gut, dyed. I saw her in earnest conversation with a PhD student who was studying grass-work.

Warren was in business mode, showing round two visitors, white men wearing ballcaps. Something told me he was seeking sponsorship, to keep the dig going.

Soon, children had taken over water-spraying duties. Two dogs scampered in, were ejected. A little girl was looking at the so-called dolls. 'Do you like them?' I asked. She replied, 'If you make these, the spirits haunt you.'

At the table given over to personal adornment were some photographs of Yup'ik people taken as recently as the 1930s – men squinting out of fur-lined parkas, their faces pierced with labrets, women with their lower lips all hanging with beads. On show was a whole tray of labrets, some two inches long, some carved with seal faces. If a seal face looks out from a man's face, is he a man or a seal? Or a touch of both, like a selkie?

The both at once. The seal/whale knife. I saw John Smith there with Sarah's brother-in-law, the town's other ivory carver, peering together at the pendant with the recurring design of concentric circles round a dot. The all-seeing eye.

I felt that the village of Quinhagak was the dot, and around it wheeled the land and animals, sea and sky.

Feelings inevitably ran high. The woman who had come to the site and spoken about names was saying, 'We need to get our history back! The Pilgrim Fathers never *discovered* America!'

Someone else said, 'You know the church owns the land between here and the river? They should give it back. They can keep their church and the graveyard, but they should give us back the land. That would be a *gesture*.'

A man I knew as Willard said, 'It's getting better. More education. We've got kids going to college, taking leadership roles. They're out-migrating but contributing. We've still got poverty, unemployment ... We want to live a subsistence life but we have to negotiate with the world out there. We've got to think about the carrying capacity of the land, and the cost of fuel...'

Hunter-gatherers who stop at the store on the way home.

'You've got your land,' I said. 'So much depends on that. Where I come from, land's almost all in private hands.'

'One hundred and thirty thousand acres.' He smiled. 'Yes, it's for everyone. There's interesting stuff happening, with Native land claims.'

When everyone had gone home, the marathon of packing away resumed. Into big plastic trunks, suitable for airfreight, went all the artefacts, the soil samples, the wood and fauna samples. There would be forty-five crates to ship to Aberdeen.

There was an end-of-term feeling that night, with everyone in good humour, and relieved. Mike Smith and his friend Walter came to join the students for the evening, to enjoy the company of youngsters their own age. The place became a clutter again, like student digs. They hooked up a laptop and a screen, got on to Netflix, pulled up chairs and prepared to watch *Game of Thrones*. The opening scenes showed snow falling. Snow on snow.

Before that, though, I asked Mike if he'd mind telling me his Yup'ik name.

'Sure. *Kisngalria*. Kis-ngal-ggia. It means "One who has sunken." Also, *Alaskuk*, A-luss-kook. I'll write it for you. And *Atlgan*. That's Atll-ggun. They were two people who died around the time I was born.'

Walter said: 'I'm *Qaqatak*...'

'I know that word! That's...'

'Common Loon.'

A boy who is a bird. I looked at Walter in delight. *Qaqatak*. I wanted to run round everyone I'd met, asking them all. Every Sarah and Mary. Every Smith and Jones.

John Smith was *Dunreeluk*. 'It means,' he said diffidently, 'something to do with light.'

Later Melia said: 'Did you hear John saying that his grandfather was a shaman? Twenty years ago, no one would have admitted to that. They wouldn't have spoken about it. They'd have been ashamed.'

The reporter wrote a long and supportive feature, but her paper hadn't been able to resist using the word 'treasure.' When he saw it, Rick growled through his beard, 'This is not about *treasure*. This is about cultural resilience.'

It's about saying, this is yours. Everything you feared you'd lost, or never even knew you had. Look. It's here. It's back.

* * *

The 'bow and arrow wars' were resolved by dancing. That's the story. A realisation came that war and terror were futile, and that competition could be carried out by other means. By dance. Singing. Feasting – and naming. I was told that the communities bound themselves together again by naming. A baby born on one 'side' of the conflict would be named for a deceased person on the other. They had dance festivals.

* * *

'He who loses his language loses his world.' So wrote the Gaelic poet Iain Crichton Smith/Iain Mac a'Ghobhainn. One wonders if the converse is true. If one loses one's world, one loses one's language. The world of things, of

making, of the land and animals and the stories and the
hands' work.

The day after the 'show and tell,' almost our last
day in Quinhagak, another quieter event was held.
An anthropologist called Ann Fienup-Riordan had
arrived. Petite, in her sixties, fearless, Ann was well
known and well liked by the Quinhagak folk. She had
learned Yup'ik, and spent her professional life speaking
and documenting stories and histories, and editing
books like *Erinaput Unguvaniartut* (*So Our Voices Will
Live*) and *Quinhagak History and Oral Traditions*. In her
books there are many headings like:

> *Travelling in the wilderness.*
> *She said if a red fox had crossed somewhere,*
>   *that area was safe.*
> *They say only the south wind flattens grass.*
> *We are teachers to our grandchildren.*
> *Lead dogs are very smart.*
> *Squirrel hunting in the mountains.*
> *A story of when the ice detached and people floated away.*

Ann had come to talk again to elders whom she knew,
elders who spoke little if any English. In a comfortably
furnished room across the yard next to the supermarket,
a room with sofas and a stove, another pot of broth was
set to cook, and some equipment arranged: a sound
recorder and a video camera. Into the room, carefully
assisted up the external stairs, came three of the town's
oldest folks – two men and a woman in their eighties,
all wrinkle-faced. They sat at a table. The window gave

views of the tundra and distant mountains they had known all their long lives. Snacks were provided; the elders all were keen on cartons of fruit juice.

I sat quietly on a sofa at the back of the room, ready to listen, though I knew I would understand nothing. It was the first time I'd heard Yup'ik spoken in a sustained way. That was the point. The elders were here to discuss objects found on the site. In this way, more would be known about the objects, and the objects would reawaken the elders' language as they turned the objects in their old hands.

The eldest man was brown as a nut. His eyes were narrow and his face deeply lined after a lifetime in the light and snow. He wore a sweatshirt so thick and brown, you could have mistaken it for hide. He looked just like the men in the photographs, his grandfather's generation, minus only the labrets.

When the elders were settled and the tape running, Ann brought in a tray of half a dozen objects and set it on the table. Unlike in Kim's Game, the objects remained in view. This was a test of memory of a different order. One by one, one at a time, the elders took up the objects. Their fingers were thick. They had known much work and many winters.

On the first tray were snare-pins, root-picks, a bucket handle. Everyday objects. They turned the objects, felt and examined them, and begin to speak. Explanations, lore, stories. Ann was there to understand, guide, clarify. The bucket handle was made of bentwood; the root-picks, which women would have used to dig for edible roots, were made from the ribs of sea mammals.

The language was soothing. The elders spoke softly, making sounds like wood gently knocked on wood. Through the window, a green rib of tundra, a wall of mountains. The objects were turned, demonstrated. The last time they had been touched by Yup'ik hands and named like this was five hundred years ago.

From time to time a phrase was translated into English, for clarification. An antler scraper. 'To take the fat off the skin?' 'Yes, like this.' Now they were examining a stone pick, weighing it, testing its edge. They identified the source of that particular kind of stone, a particular valley in the mountains.

Out the window, a flight of geese passed, the grasses rippled. It would soon rain. The eldest man had the stone pick in one hand as he reached for a chocolate cookie with the other. I was listening to the language of this landscape, as expressed with the hands and eye. The sun had favoured a few clouds over the mountains. The broth simmered.

'This is from a woman's toolbox. Knives, needles, thimbles. They'd keep them close by.'

The objects are out of the earth, back in the hands of people who call them into memory and know them, weigh them, test them, name them. Truly, they have come home.

* * *

It was time to leave. But before that the site had to be backfilled, and closed down for winter.

In the last few days, I walked, knowing I'd never see anywhere so spacious and so radiant again.

That's okay. I wished the Quinhagak people well.

I wish them their reclaimed past.

I wish them a future. I wish them snow.

Intending to head to the shore, I walked out along toward the three turbines, and there through my binoculars watched a big flight of geese coming in, and a jaeger hovering like a kestrel. Closer, a large mammal made me pause. *I'm here!* But it was just a village dog.

The turbines' columns made strange fluty sounds. A duck quacked from some hidden pool.

I wanted to sit a while and look out to sea, in hopes of seeing beluga whales, because if you don't look, you don't see, and I was going home soon.

Out across the Bering Sea, a vapour trail.

At the spot Sarah had brought me on her four-wheeler, I sat on a tussock and looked out, now with binoculars, now with my naked eye. The tide was coming in, white horses in the distance. The river flowed to my right, leftwards lay the miles of shore down to the site, where the heavy work of backfilling was about to begin.

I sat letting my eyes sharpen, hoping for whale-blows as they chased salmon.

The ryegrass, for basketmaking, grew behind me. Sand with pebbles and feathers.

A couple of pacific loons riding on the water.

Then, coming down the riverside, there appeared a four-wheeler. It was driven by John Smith. In his blue, thick-checked shirt and windblown hair, I realised I'd never seen him outdoors before.

'I'm looking for animals,' I said. 'And birds.' A natural and unembarrassing thing to do. 'Beluga whales.'

'Yes, they come by. Chasing the herring-fish. Mostly in spring. We harpoon them! They're tough. Good for the teeth.'

'Are you going somewhere?' I asked.

'Just out for a look around.'

Like Sarah had been, and Warren had done, up on the bluff upriver. Janitors of a huge, open-air domain.

This business of looking at the land – no one says, 'Come on, hurry up, what are you looking at?'

'What's that?' John asked, pointing. He had good eyesight, for a man of seventy who wears glasses, with the optician an aircraft flight away.

'A gull. See.' I handed over my binoculars. John checked the gull, then began slowly panning the sea.

'My, these are good! Ha! I just came out for a look-see, and I found a shaman! Seeing far, far...' He gestured toward the horizon.

'Nah,' I laughed. 'They're just half-decent binoculars...'

'There were women shamans, you know. Stronger than the men, some of them. They could put you in a trance!'

He handed the glasses back.

'And could you get out of the trance?'

He made a strange gesture. This man who could mimic sandhill cranes and owls was doing something odd with his hands. Weaving and catching. 'You had to *find* your way out.'

In the silence of the shore, the strange light, it discomfited me. Frightening people, shamans.

'There were good shamans, too,' said John, reading my thoughts.

'Are there any nowadays?'

He considered.

'No. But there are people with strong minds who might want to do you harm.'

'John, what do you think will happen, in the future?'

It was a while before he answered.

'I hope snow. The grasses are long.'

'Is that a sign of snow to come, long grasses?'

'In what way, the future?'

'I mean the land. Animals. People. Yup'ik people. Climate change.'

'I don't concern myself much with people. The animals ... We are conserving now, caribou, fish – that's good. We'll adapt. We'll expect the unexpected. Mother nature will do what she will do.'

'If anyone adapts, you people will.'

He smiled at me. 'We watch you people on TV!'

'And what do you think of us people on TV?'

'We watch you running about wild!'

'Come and see what we're really like. Come to Scotland.'

'By dog team!' he said.

'Smart ones!' I laughed.

'Which way do I go?'

I pointed east, upriver. But I could equally have pointed west, over the Bering Sea, to Siberia. Just keep going.

* * *

By Labor Day it was cool in the mornings and, as Mike noted, the swallows were gone. I walked to the end of the street, to where the tundra opened. I wanted to remember how the tundra grasses rippled, how the light, so radiant, fell from the sky. I passed a discarded freezer full of garbage bags, and some playful puppy dogs. Then a little girl ran up to me. She had something exciting to tell: 'There's a Big Foot!'

'Where!'

'Upriver! My dad saw it. He's got a photo. It's got four toes!'

'I'd love to see the photo,' I said, but already she was gone, running up the stairs and into her house – the one with whalebones and an upturned snowmobile outside.

The shore was empty. Silent. Again the tide was out, as it had been the first time I came here. Unutterably silent, shining. It still unnerved me. Tyre tracks on the dark sand, and miles of emptiness. I walked down toward the site, then stopped, suddenly unsure. What to do? Walk to the site? Go back into the village? Might there be bears? There had been no mention of bears lately.

I walked south along the silent shore. It was too quiet.

In the distance, a movement. Something on the beach. I watched, squinting. Not a bear, not a woman, not a raven. It was a four-wheeler, of course. Actually, two four-wheelers, heading toward me at speed, churning clouds of sand.

Soon they were on me, but they slowed and I recognised the four village lads hired as labourers to help with the backfilling. They were heading home for lunch.

They stopped.

'You wanna ride?'

Choices, choices. A last, solitary walk by the silent shore of the Bering Sea, or a lift with these diffident handsome Yup'ik boys?

I was old enough to be their mother.

The sea shone, the sky was vast. I'd never be here again.

'Sure,' I said. 'Why not?'

The Eagle

A SHAPE IN THE AIR above the ridge has caught my attention and, rather than drive squinting upwards through the windscreen, I pull over at the next passing place and switch off the engine.

It's summer, a long July gloaming. The road I'm taking cuts through a rough glen. There are no houses on this stretch, only the thin road and a lochan of peat-coloured water. The hill on the left is a steep strew of bare rock and heather rising to a ridge which runs north for about a mile and a half; the hill on the right is lower. The whole glen, now I've stopped, has become a place of entrancing desolation.

I leave the car, feel the breeze and look up. Maybe it's just a buzzard and you know what they say – if you're asking yourself, 'Is that an eagle or a buzzard?' then it's a buzzard. Ninety-eight per cent of all eagles are buzzards. But there's something in the authoritative way the bird is occupying airspace, a black hyphen above the near-bare crest of the hill.

Now the bird is joined by another, at a distance, and the two of them are dark against the evening sky. The two are in relationship, you can sense it, but not obviously acknowledging each other.

I have the first in the binoculars now: yes, the long, straight underside of the wings, the deep indentations, spikes almost, of the wing tips. It shows no colour except the back of the head or nape, which is markedly pale, and which now and again ignites in the evening light. But I have to look hard to see that. I lower the glasses and watch both together, a team. What marks them out is the way they treat the air: as a resource, a birthright, theirs in never-ending abundance.

Now one peels off and glides down into the glen on the far side of the ridge and is gone from view. In its absence, the first eagle flies lower down toward the valley floor here where the road runs, where I stand leaning against the car. This bird is hanging in the air on one side of the hill, its mate like a counterweight on the other.

Because it's dropped height, it's not now a shape exposed against the sky but a movement camouflaged against the heather and bracken of the hillside. It's consequently difficult to follow, until it turns and for a moment displays the brassy colour of its back. I realise that, in all the time since I left the car, it has not once beaten its wings.

Down here at the roadside the ground is damp, bog cotton shivers. No other vehicle has passed. Over this landscape the eagle moves as though the air were ice; as if it were a puck sliding over ice.

For a moment there I lost the eagle, but now it's visible again. It's coming closer and looks as though it might pass almost directly overhead. I try to keep track of it in the binoculars, and sure enough it descends at a long angle, flies across the road and glides toward the lower reaches of the hill on the other side. This would be a journey of about a kilometre on the ground – a stumbling ankle-twisting walk it would be, too. Now it's swinging round and in turning shows a mantle of colour on its upper side, more brassy than golden. It's obtained some updraft from somewhere and slides up the air again, as though riding an invisible escalator. At last, when it must feel itself about to stall, it makes four quick deep wing-beats, and carries on.

Weeks later, I ask an acquaintance who is a glider pilot about the feel of air. Are there really different textures of air, and can you feel them? 'Oh, yes, yes, yes!' she says. Even encased in a glider? 'Certainly,' she says. 'It's as different as a road surface changing as you drive, and as sudden. You feel it through your body, the glider feels it, having no engines, nothing to propel you through...'

Then, unprompted, she says, 'I often imagine what it must be like for the big birds. Like eagles, who feel the air so much more than we do, much more sensitive. You know how they loop round and round, feeling out the thermals that will lift them? It must be like swimming in a lake, bathing now in warmth, now in coolness...'

I'm still leaning against the car, and until now had the first eagle in sight, in the binoculars. It was drifting along against a slope of rock and dark heather. But now I see something I hadn't noticed before. It's a shed made of corrugated iron, mustard-coloured, halfway up the hill. It's enclosed in a decrepit wire fence, with a lopsided sign saying, DANGER: KEEP OUT. The eagle has just passed over it, but the shed distracts me for a moment too long. What danger could there be in a ramshackle old hut? And who would go there, anyway? In that moment, in that change in the texture of my attention, a lurch like when you drive from smooth tarmac onto cobbles, I lose sight of the eagle altogether. It's vanished, its mate has vanished, and there's nothing to do but drive on.

Links of Noltland

I

Because a tractor was lumbering toward me, I'd pulled into a passing-place. It was silage-cutting time on Westray and many tractors were abroad on the island's few miles of road. The driver waved as he passed. In the lay-by, I stayed put, just looking around.

On my right, in a field behind a wire fence, a bull was chewing slowly, lost in his bull's dream. To the left, the land sloped down toward a small loch. All the land surrounding the loch was fenced with stone dykes or barbed wire, all had been turned into fields. Only the heights of the smooth hills beyond were left uncontained. Of the lower fields, some were lush with grass and held cattle, or 'kye' – farming folk here still use the old Scots word. Other fields were ripe with brittle-gold barley.

I drove on down into the town of Pierowall, a straggle of shoreside grey houses and stores. Because the tide was low, plains of bright mustard-gold seaweed were exposed, with a few seals hauled out. At the school, which was closed for the summer holiday, I turned sharp left and followed a thin road as it began to climb up over the hill to serve the last few farms on the island's west side, the side exposed to the Atlantic. Up there were cliffs and a lighthouse, then nothing else till Newfoundland, as folk are quick to tell you.

Before the hill, however, a small sign indicated a track that led to a beach. I'd been told to follow this track, so I bumped along between stone walls. Behind the walls, more pale cows were grazing, another farm with its tractor in the dungy yard.

'Links of Noltland,' the sign had said. It means something like 'the sandy dunes of the land of the cattle' in a mix of Scots, Norse and English. The car I was driving had been kindly loaned to me. It was an elderly island car but a loan nonetheless, so I drove gingerly round the potholes down to the track's end, where a white minibus was already parked. This was the edge of another bay, north-facing, a shallow half-mile of creamy sand and slabs of rock. It rose into cliffs in the eastern distance. I left the car. Big waves were driving ashore, leaving plumes of rainbow hanging in the air behind them. Heaps of tangle had been freshly delivered by the tide, but no one was collecting it. In the recent past it would have been scooped up for fertiliser; in the remote past, before peat ever formed on the hills, it would have gone for fuel.

I floundered through dry sand, past a prominent stony mound toward a gate in a wire fence. A sign on the fence, intended to explain something about the dunes behind, had itself been thoroughly sand-blasted. The gist was that the dunes were man-made, restored and planted with rye and marram grass. Beyond the fence, I could see spoil heaps and a few figures wrapped against sand and wind, intent on the ground beneath their feet. Here also was that symbol of the globalised world, the shipping container. Two shipping containers in fact, a green one and a blue, parked in the sand. The shipping containers served as office and mess-hut and store.

The Links of Noltland archaeological dig was begun almost a decade ago. Its directors are Hazel Moore and Graeme Wilson, a couple who now live on Westray and have established family life here. It was Hazel who showed me round at first, crossing the site to meet me like a moving flame. She is small of stature with coppery-bright hair that catches the sun, and very bright blue eyes. Her accent is a broad Dublin.

Hazel led me to the east side where, backed by spoil and an array of old tyres, we had an overview of the site. I saw a species of chaos, but my eye was far from attuned. Before me were sections of walling a metre high at most, freshly exposed, and stones everywhere, embedded in the earth, and wheelbarrows, buckets and string. Among the stones, eight or ten people were at work, some drawing plans, some scraping with trowels, filling buckets with the earth they'd removed. All wore jackets, most had hats of some sort, to keep their hair out of their eyes. It was August, but not balmy.

Hazel explained that a dune system which had existed for millennia had recently been obliterated by the wind. A natural cycle had been interrupted. Across a mere fifteen or twenty years the ancient dunes had collapsed, and the vegetation had vanished.

Orkney is a windy place, storms are not unknown, but the couple's interim archaeological report had called this sustained erosion 'exceptional and unprecedented.' But with the sand and vegetation scoured away, a ground surface had been exposed which had been recognised as an extensive Neolithic and Bronze Age settlement. Houses, workshops, walls, even field systems and soil, it was all here. They wouldn't last, though: having been exposed after their long burial, those remains too were immediately vulnerable to the wind.

Hazel said: 'This whole site is not going to last. And it's not just Orkney, this erosion is something we're seeing throughout Scotland. The archaeology we are digging has been buried for five thousand years, and it has never been exposed like this in all that time. What's happening is significant really to ... well, to archaeology, but also to us, the human race.'

When the scale of the site was realised, Historic Scotland commissioned excavations to record, maybe protect, what remained before it was lost. There have now been nine summers of excavations – no one could have predicted that, least of all Historic Scotland's accountants – and new features were still coming to light. The area we were looking at, six hundred square metres, was only a fraction of the whole.

The working site had a raw, slightly wounded look, like skin after you peel off a sticking plaster. Other parts of the Links were protected under black plastic sheeting weighed down by tyres and stones. The sections under wraps were mostly of the Bronze Age, as was the big mound on the shore. The exposed areas which were being worked at present were Neolithic. People had lived here, developing and changing and toughing it out, for a very long time. As Graeme said later, as far as people were concerned, the Links were a very successful wee bit of Orkney landscape.

Hazel led me round, introducing me to the team as they worked. In truth I saw their motley garments before I registered their faces, as they unbent from the ground: earth-caked jeans and fluorescent jackets, knitted headbands and piratical scarves, everyone seemed weather-worn under the Orkney light and salt winds. Archaeologists are accustomed to appraising what turns up; I felt duly appraised.

It appears that the first farmers had built a hefty enclosing wall and, within it, several discrete houses with various yards and passageways and 'activity areas.' Or maybe not. It's possible the few houses came first, and at some early point a wall was built around them. Either way, having defined their space, the people just kept building on top of it.

'How many layers of occupation have you gone down already?' I asked Hazel, and she sucked in her breath.

'A simple answer? Three or four layers, within the enclosure. A metre and a half in depth. But they didn't raze the place then start again. Buildings just fell out of use, or were closed, or robbed of stone or reinvented and rebuilt. It was in use for about seven hundred years.'

In brief, as Graeme put it later, with Links of Noltland, they have a second chance at Skara Brae. That Neolithic village was excavated in the 1930s, but not before it had been plundered. Links of Noltland was a bigger settlement: here were homes, field systems, boundaries. 'Everything that was chucked away at Skara Brae, or not recognised, we have here.'

Skara Brae is hugely famous now, with a visitor centre and reconstructions and all. If a couple of big cruise liners are in port, so many buses take visitors there that they have to drive around in circles till a parking place becomes available. Or so it's said.

But Links doesn't look like Skara Brae, with its manicured grass and made paths and interpretation panels. At least, not yet.

This season the team was concentrating on three or four houses, early ones. With expert eyes, and deft use of trowel and brush, they could tell one house from another, and identify the Neolithic fads and changes of mind. They could here, too, discern the homely features that make Skara Brae so popular: each house has an entranceway, a central hearth and often a 'dresser,' or stone shelves facing the entrance.

Some even have covered drains leading out of the house under the wall. Drains, conducting water and waste, or alternatively flues, bringing air into the fire. It's one of the many small mysteries, hard to tell because, as Hazel said, they seem to have been all intention, but never actually used.

We toured the site, stepping stone to stone, clay floor to clay floor. Stones and bone. In one house, I was aghast to see the orange earth of a hearth being trowelled away. A Neolithic hearth! But I was told not to worry, they were certain there was another, older one beneath.

At lunchtime, when the day had warmed, everyone downed tools and retired to the shipping containers to eat. We left the Neolithic and sat among the detritus of our own age. The mess-hut had a gathering of picnic chairs and upturned buckets, but because it was warm, people preferred to lie on the sand looking at the clouds, or read books, or moan about the complete lack of mobile signal because the island's only mast was being repaired. One digger, Emily, had mastered the art of sitting in a tilted wheelbarrow as though it was an armchair. They were robust, good-humoured people. You'd have to be, to live as they do.

The ten or so employees on the site are all professionals, there were no undergraduate students or volunteers. Several held PhDs, some had been coming here to Westray every summer for years. By chance, half were Irish. Irish accents predominated across the site. One of them told me Links was a 'godsend,' graduate jobs being so hard to find. But it does mean they live an itinerant life often into their thirties or forties, with months spent in rented rooms or holiday lets, with the same people at home as they work with. They all have worst-house-you've-ever-lived-in tales. They are all quick to laugh.

I admitted I was confused by the site, despite Hazel's tour. So many stones! But the archaeologists just laughed. 'Join the club!' They said. 'Us too!'

The midday sky was clear, but for one cavalcade of clouds over the sea. Directly above a kittiwake passed, bright white, rimmed with light.

* * *

Graeme is calm of manner and less voluble than Hazel. His concern of the moment was the enclosing wall. After the lunch break he took over from Hazel and showed me how this wall had been traced and exposed around two thirds of the site. It was almost a metre wide, two skins of stone packed with a core of clay. In places it stood intact a few courses high; in others it seemed just a strew of rubble. Where it had been excavated, you could admire its sharp Neolithic stonework, clean and unweathered, having been buried so long. The stone was the reddish island sandstone, lovely for building with, and the Neolithic masons had taken care, especially on the exterior. The wall had been made to impress anyone approaching it from outside.

'Impress who?' I asked.

'Ah, well,' said Graeme.

In other parts the wall had collapsed, and you could walk on its remains as if it was a crazy-paving garden path. On the east side was a clear breach, the entranceway into the huddle of buildings. On the west, however, this enclosure wall vanished. It looked as though it was continuing outwith the site. Today, this was the job in hand. One of the excavating team, Dan O'Meara, had dug a trial trench where he suspected the wall might run, and sure enough, when he got down deep enough, there it was looking up at him. The problem was, if it followed its arc, the wall would be continuing under the site's spoil heaps, something that couldn't have been foreseen back when work began.

Graeme had arranged for a local farmer to come with a small JCB to bulldoze away those spoil heaps, so they could excavate underneath, find this enclosure wall, complete its circle and finally get the full measure of the Neolithic settlement. Furthermore, if the wall ran where expected, Graeme postulated that there would be room enough within its embrace for two more houses, or structures of some sort, also presently buried.

'Isn't that exciting?' I asked. Well, yes, of course. But new developments were also a bit of a headache. Historic Scotland had told the Links team repeatedly that this season must be the last. There could be no more funding – not least because Historic Scotland no longer existed as an entity. The Scottish government had amalgamated it with another body to form Historic Environment Scotland, presumably to save money.

'They've said that before, though, about the funding. More than once. But this time they seem to mean it.'

'So what will happen? It won't just be covered in sand again, will it?'

By accident or design we had worked our way right round the site, and were back by the shipping containers. The blue one was stamped with a logo of an eagle bearing an anchor, with 'United States Customs.' How do these things get here, on a beach on Westray?

Hazel was within at a makeshift desk, doing paperwork. 'No,' she said. 'It won't be covered in sand. It would be safe if it was packed with sand. It will just be destroyed by the wind.'

Graeme said, 'But for now, if there are new structures, our job is to excavate them, so we'll just get on with it.'

That was a phrase I heard several times over the next couple of weeks. If I asked how life was for people in the Neolithic or Bronze Age, chances are I'd receive the reply: 'People just got on with it. They didn't know they were Neolithic or Bronze Age.'

In the spirit of 'getting on with it,' I took from the green shipping container a spare trowel, bucket and kneeling mat, because trowelling is hard on the knees. Graeme despatched me to the site's west side, the side with the emerging wall and still-hidden structures, to help do preparatory work before the arrival of the JCB.

The weather was lovely by then, the island skies vast, its low green hills scattered with farmsteads. People had even taken their coats off. I spent the afternoon trowelling back a 'deposition layer' with Anna Maria Diana of Sicily, who had just completed her PhD in human osteoarchaeology. Anna had studied in Edinburgh, so we had that city in common to talk about as we trowelled out

earth and occasional pieces of pottery or flint, which we
had to bag and label as 'small finds.'

It's a good way to have conversations, side by side,
concentrating on another task. Anna was half-Italian,
half-Romanian, and spoke both, and also perfect, Italian-
accented English. We chatted about various Edinburgh
cafes where she'd worked, and the city's mouse-infested
tenements.

We scraped away until larger stones began to reveal
themselves. It seemed an incoherent spread of stones,
but when Graeme came by on his director's rounds, he
said, 'Looks like you've got something here.'

'Really?'

He pointed with his trowel, 'Coming round here...'

I liked the texture of flint, serious and no-nonsense,
tumbling under the trowel. They were little knapped-off
pieces, brownish-pink or orangey colour. The Neolithic
people probably found nodules on the shore, back then,
part of the island's bounty.

Anna said, 'I don't mind not finding anything much.
I enjoy the colours of the earth. The smell of the earth.
But not this dung-smell!'

It was true, there was a dung-smell. The farmer on the
hill was spraying his fields. We could straighten up and
watch the red tractor and trailer climb the small field,
turn, then process down again.

Personally, I thought the smell was quite funny, as
we trowelled away. Appropriate. A sort of scratch'n'sniff
archaeology. In its Neolithic day, the whole place would
have reeked of dung and smoke.

'And smelly humans,' said Anna.

'What do you think this settlement was like?' I asked her. 'In its time, five thousand years ago?'

'Gorgeous, I think. I envy them.'

'But they died young?'

'On average. Almost everyone had arthritis by their twenties.'

'I find it hard to believe, that people died so soon.'

Working like this meant kneeling with our backs to the sea. On a calm day, you could forget it was there, except when you stood, stiffly, to empty a bucket or barrow. Then you could see the ocean, all the way to the northern horizon, with gannets diving and a lobster boat working the creels.

* * *

I'd been offered a rented room in a fine tall house on the far side of the island. The house stood where the road ended, almost on a promontory. Hundreds of years old, it was grey with crow-stepped gables, and ought to have been the epitome of Scottish gloom. But it was warm and light, with solid old-fashioned mahogany furniture. There were chandeliers and a doll's house, a piano and a huge dining-room table.

Many nine-pane windows gave views to all sides, and just outside, under the shelter of stone dykes, grew those white dog roses with thick leaves you get at the coast. A donkey grazed in a paddock, and beyond the paddock wall the land sloped greenly down three-quarters of a mile toward the Westray Firth, with other islands rising beyond.

In a work of love and great spirit, Sandy and Willie McEwen had restored the place from a ghostly, roofless wreck. Twenty-first-century interventions, a wind turbine and ground-source system, provided the heat and electric light. For the first time in its long life, the house was not damp. It was as though the house had been built three hundred years before the technology arrived that would allow it to flourish.

'Do you see that mound there?' Sandy had stopped beside me at the window. She was petite, with a thick plait of grey hair. 'At the land's end?'

'I see it.'

'It's an Iron Age burial mound. It's on an islet. There were over a hundred skeletons in there, many babies. It was being eroded away, so they excavated it. That's how I met Hazel and Graeme. I liked them. They were respectful of the babies. It was a prehistoric cemetery for hundreds of years. Then the Vikings came and put a fishing station on it.'

Sandy and her husband are Quakers. 'We had this house blessed by eight different kinds of faith,' she said.

'I can sense that,' I said. 'It feels fine.'

It became my habit to oscillate back and forth across the island, from the wuthering heights of West Manse to the blown sands of Links of Noltland. Sometimes I drove, sometimes cycled. The skies were huge, there were cattle in the fields, and flocks of common gulls and starlings, wagtails and pipits on the road. I learned where the flocks of sparrows lived, and which rough fields were favoured by curlew. Most of the farms and houses were inhabited, but a few were derelict. Daily my eye was drawn to one particularly grand farmhouse on a hill, or rather its south-facing walled garden, an island rarity. The house was clearly long abandoned, and the garden now sheltered the island's only woodland, an acre of tight-packed, wind-sculpted sycamores.

Each of the small Neolithic houses within the enclosure wall was the property, so to speak, of one archaeologist. There was Maeve's house, Dawn's house, Emily's house and Lesley's. Each knew her own intimately as she worked round and down, excavating and planning.

The next day, keen to make more sense of the site, I walked round having a word with each householder. The same phrases recurred.

'To see how this relates.'

'To find out what's going on.'

'Then, this can come out.'

'This house is early in the sequence, we're getting new kinds of flint.' New meaning older.

Dawn Gooney was working on a house in the middle of the enclosure. She is an expert on bone, and had been working on the site for several seasons. Today she was drawing an inner corner by the entrance to her house where it was obvious, even to me, that alterations had taken place. The doorway was clearly defined in stone, three or four courses high, with sharp corners because the original building had been almost cruciform. But someone had taken a notion to fill in the corners, so making the inner space more rounded. This more recent Neolithic stonework wasn't up to the standard of the original; you could tell where one ended and the other began. Having drawn it and photographed it thoroughly, Dawn would soon begin to take out the amendment, and reveal the sharper, original stonework behind.

'I like this kind of thing,' she said, kneeling on the ground, a black band keeping her hair out of her eyes. 'I'm practical-minded myself, and I like seeing someone else's mind at work, having these same thoughts thousands of years ago. It's as if the daughter-in-law moved in and wanted to put her stamp on it. Let's get rid of these gloomy corners!'

Also, someone, sometime, five millennia ago, had decided the floor needed re-laying. The old one was too rough and dirty, too full of rubbish and bone.

He or she had fetched the right kind of clay from across the island and packed a new floor in over the old one, and then, in the centre, had dug slots to accommodate stone kerbs a few inches high, which would define the fireplace. He'd dug a slot, inserted a long stone, decided he didn't like it, removed it and back-filled the slot to take another, shorter stone. To Dawn's eye, the actions were as specific and identifiable as that. A couple of hours' work, one day very long ago.

I say 'he,' because when these stones had been planned, photographed and were ready for removal, the task fell to the strongest men, Dan or Criostoir usually. They'd heave them across the site to the spoil heaps, and toss them aside, your Neolithic handiwork gone.

The problem, Dawn said, was the dating. Without organic material for carbon-dating, it's hard to tell how much time had passed between one modification and another. It might indeed have been the daughter-in-law, or centuries may have gone by. The place might have been a ruin before someone else moved in and rebuilt.

Whatever the time frame, these long-ago alterations and changes – grand restorations or fiddling about – were domestic. What seemed to be emerging from this cluster of dwellings by the seashore were ordinary people's ordinary lives, hundreds of years' worth. Standing at the edge of the site, overlooking the houses, I could see a woman at work in each, crouched to the floor, or bent over a board. So much bending and hauling and kneeling and stooping and lifting.

It was Dawn who was removing the hearth; fire-blackened, long-buried earth peeled away under her trowel. But underneath, she was sure, lay the more ancient stain of an older hearth, the older floor.

The original architecture is muscular, too. Like the enclosure wall, the house walls also had two skins of stone and a filling of clay. No wind or weather would penetrate them. They must have been silent inside, except for the fire spitting, movement, voices. And coughing, in the rank smoke.

* * *

Despite Links of Noltland being difficult to reach, every day brought visitors to the site. If they come by ferry, it's a ninety-minute sailing from Kirkwall, then a further seven miles across the island from the ferry pier. There is no bus to Links, and no taxis on the island, but nonetheless, two or three or four or five parties could arrive on any given day, walking up from the beach, entering through the ineffective gate and making their way up to the site.

Graeme or Hazel would stop what they were doing to explain the site, making a slow tour of the perimeter with the interested parties. Most left enthused, but the team told me they had once had a visitor who declared it was 'all impossible – because people were monkeys then, five thousand years ago.'

One afternoon an elderly couple made their way up from the beach slowly through the soft sand to the site's edge. As was often the case, they were retirees, holiday-makers with the means to follow their interests into their sixties, seventies, even eighties. After Hazel had explained to them what was going on, they worked their way round the perimeter of the site to where I was standing, still trying to get my eye in.

They were Australian, and the man was on a senti-mental journey. He joined me overlooking the site, watching the archaeologists, but what he wanted to talk about was his own family. He was tall, rheumy-eyed, and he told me his forebears had come from Westray. To be precise, his great-great-grandfather had left the island in 1870, at age nineteen.

He had never been here before, but he had asked around and found, been shown, actually been to visit, the very cottage his forebear had left. 'See...' – he held out his camera so that I could see a photo of a typical nineteenth-century island two-room but and ben. Its original roof, probably flagstones, had been replaced with one of corrugated iron, its windows were broken, but nonetheless it was the croft on the hill, and it was still there.

'That's wonderful,' I said. 'Thrilling to have found it...'

'It was easy. I asked the islanders. They just said, "Huh, you're one o' them. That was their house up there..." We even saw the pier he had sailed from...'

Then the woman spoke. 'And now we're at the other side of the planet.'

She looked at the Neolithic houses which had lain cold in the ground these five thousand years, now in the process of being dug out. Perhaps a frisson about time and its passing touched her, because she said, 'We don't live long, do we?'

At tea break I told the archaeologists about the Australian man seeking his ancestral home, but they just laughed.

'I bet they send everyone to the same old house ... Look! This was your grandaddy's,' said Criostoir.

'I bet it's for sale!' said Emily.

Later a group of three English women arrived, determinedly wearing flowery summer skirts. 'Oh,' they said, 'we live here now, on Westray.'

Half the island's population are incomers, mostly from England. It's English accents you hear in the shops and hotel bar. Because of this influx, Westray's population has risen to seven hundred, following a slump that imperilled the school and shops.

'Visitors think it's lovely and wild,' said Graeme later, 'but it's a monoculture.'

'You mean the farms? All the beef cattle?'

'They do one thing, but they do it well. There's less diversity, even since we came here. Fewer tattie patches, less arable. Since the new ro-ro ferry came, people can easily get to Tesco in Kirkwall.'

At the end of the day, Graeme stood at the theodolite, as he did every afternoon, to note the position of the finds. Numbers are called: *3015 flint, 3016 flint, 3017 pot.* Occasionally *ochre* or *rose quartz*. The finds are taken in plastic bags to await their journey to the store, where they will wait again until the excavation is over and the long 'post-ex' business of analysis and study begins. Well, they've waited long enough anyway, the flints and bones, for their moment of fame.

After the finds were noted, at about ten to five, he gave the nod and trowels were thrown into buckets, buckets piled onto wheelbarrows and trundled round to the site hut.

No one hung about on site any longer than they had to, except Graeme himself, who remained standing in the middle of the enclosure, in his blue coat and woolly hat, looking pensive.

'What are you thinking?' I asked.

'It's all a bit confusing. It's not coming together yet.'

'Will it?'

'It'll have to! Else ... we'll just have to forget about it.'

* * *

The evenings were long and light, so usually I went out.
I took myself down a sandy path between fields toward
another bay, a sheltered one called the Mae Sands.

Inevitably, a few cows grazed and a gang of ravens
called to each other and tumbled in the air. In rare places
where no cattle could reach, like the verges of the little
path, there grew purple knapweed, yarrow, self-heal, and
orange bees foraged.

The path opened onto a half-mile of sand curving
away eastward, with a wall of dunes behind. On the sand
grew clumps of sea-rocket, which were in flower. It was so
calm, their faint perfume scented the beach, while sand
formed sculptural vanes on the plants' downwind side. At
the strandline, turnstones worked over the weed, and a
party of sanderlings scuttled away from each new shallow
wave. Seals watched from the water, two or three.

Being on site often left me freighted with thoughts
about time, how it seems to expand and contract. I kept
having to remind myself of the ages that passed during
what we call the Neolithic or the Bronze Age. How
those people's days were as long and vital as ours.

I tried to picture that pioneer generation, landing on
a lonely shore with provisions stowed and live animals
tethered in the bottom of their boats. Sheep under a net,
seed corn and tools, the transforming 'Neolithic package'

that had been pushing across Europe for a couple of thousand years before it reached here. It was a way of life that bound you inescapably.

But does it matter, how it began? What Links reveals is the long and various 'middles,' the daily getting on with it that most of us inhabit, if we're fortunate enough to live in times of peace.

Was there peace? They'd found no evidence of real conflict or warfare. But they had discovered a body roughly buried, a body without a head.

'You wonder what transgression that was...' Graeme said mildly.

* * *

On site, where Anna and I were still trowelling away our 'deposition layer,' I cleaved to the idea of the encircling wall, because it was simple and a boundary. There were structures outside the wall which had already been excavated, other houses, Bronze Age things, but for now the enclosure helped me to understand the site. Within the wall, the village. Beyond the wall, beyond the pale – there was the wild unknown.

Hazel had made a remark that stayed with me. She had said that the early Neolithic farmers were only a step away from the wild, and they knew it. I began to wonder what it might have meant to them then, back when 'wild' was a new idea. Did stories linger of a way of life before farming, before cattle raising and sheep? Did 'the wild' thrill them, darkly? Shame them?

Arrowheads had been found on the site; people still went hunting. An intrigue had arisen about deer because deer-bones had also been found – whole skeletons, in fact. But there are no deer on the island now; it's too farmed, too small. It's possible that deer might have been imported by Neolithic people and set free to roam the still-wild hinterland, occasionally to be hunted. But mostly they were cattle-rearing folk, and how.

Some years ago, the team found cows' skulls set into the walls of a largish building, set slightly apart from the houses. Built into the fabric of its wall was a complete ring of cattle skulls, all placed upside down, with the horns facing into the room. Then the wall was built up over them, and clay packed on top, so they were no longer visible. But presumably their presence was felt by those who used the space.

'What did it mean?' I asked. 'A mass slaughter? Some kind of grand sacrifice?'

'No,' said Hazel. 'Why would you do that? It would be suicidal to slaughter all those beasts at once, if you couldn't preserve the meat. No, the dating has shown that these cattle had died, or had been slaughtered, over a span of two hundred years. The skulls must have been collected...'

'Curated' was Graeme's word.

'... accumulated in some way before the building was made, and then inserted.'

'You mean, a collection must have been built up over several generations, and then built into a wall?'

'They must have had symbolic or aesthetic significance.'

Hazel and Graeme were in the shipping container that served them as a site office, files and stores around them. Insurance documents pinned to the wall, the number of the island surgery. Hazel went on, 'I think they just had a collection they didn't know what to do with. Too many to keep, too precious to throw away. You know what it's like. So this was a solution.'

I'd begun to understand that, although Hazel and Graeme didn't agree on everything, their general attitude was like this. An Occam's razor. Don't reach for a flamboyant interpretation when a more straightforward one would do. There are other Neolithic sites all over Europe, even on Orkney, where cattle skulls have been discovered in prominent positions or in great number. Sometimes the rush to publicise has meant garish headlines. Huge sacrificial feasts are invoked, with spectacle and conspicuous consumption.

'But you think they simply kept the skulls of their cattle – or some of them, at least – and then eventually they just had to de-clutter?'

'Remember,' said Graeme, 'these animals would have had biographies.'

'What do you mean?'

'They would have been known as individuals. As personalities. Spoken about.'

'Named?'

'Maybe.'

'You think they revered their cows?'

'Worshipped!' Hazel laughed.

And loved their horns. It is possible that the Links people managed their cattle herds, and favoured a 'wild' look. They liked big bulk, and long horns, and to get that, there is some suggestion, yet to be fully explored, that they'd breed a wild aurochs into their herd now and again. Aurochs were massive wild cattle, now extinct. If someone wanted an aurochs, he'd have to catch it, albeit a calf, from mainland Scotland, truss it in a boat and bring it over the Pentland Firth, then island-hop it back to Westray. No mean feat, if that was how it was done. And all because the Links people loved the sight of horned cattle, because cattle were their pride and joy. If that was how it was. At the moment, this was just a hint among bits of bone, a speculation among skulls.

* * *

Sometimes, on my evening outings, I cycled the last mile of road on the south side, near to the marvellous house where I had my room. The road climbed a short steep hill, passing an open byre where a hundred starlings roosted, and some fields where cows grazed, then ran on along a hillside before ending in a yard. From the road-end you could walk all the way to the lighthouse on its cliffs.

A particular breeze-block shed usually gave shelter from the wind and I liked to hunker there and look for birds. It always took me a while to settle. After a day spent in company concentrating on a square of ancient earth, it was a shock to be alone in the vast moment of now.

Before me was the shining Firth; sometimes the sea roared. A kestrel often hunted the shoreline there, and one evening, when the tide was high and waves were washing onto the rocks, and a flock of curlew was sleeping out of the waves' reach, I saw a swallow leave. The swallow was just a flicker of dark that caught my eye. It ventured out from the land, directly southward over the waves, and was at once lost to view, so brave and small.

Mostly what I noticed, however, was dereliction. The new farm buildings didn't interest me; the breeze-block barn just kept the wind off, but increasingly I noticed old byres and ruined but and bens, and those odd corners where farmers threw worn-out tyres and pallets and bits of broken machinery.

There was one particular row of long-abandoned cottages guarded by nettles, which I passed on this outing. The roofs were all but gone, and through glass-less windows I saw fireplaces, and patches of distressed green paint on architraves. Junk and lumber, all lit through holes in the roof. At one door stood a tank made of flagstones in the island manner. They tugged at the heart, these places. Where had the people gone? Maybe a half-mile away, maybe Australia.

I noted a tractor so long forsaken that grass was growing up through its engine block.

This is how it happens, I thought. This was how Links must have been, with new buildings next to old, and old ones put to new uses, then filled with junk, then cleared out again and redesigned by idealistic

descendants. Then the whole lot abandoned, and left
for thousands of years.

* * *

Soon the JCB arrived and it was bittersweet to watch
it clatter back and forth, making short work of the
spoil heaps. It was a small orange machine driven by a
neighbouring farmer, and with a few deft scoops it shifted
all the spoil, along with an underlying layer of vegetation
and sand, dumping it all back against the chain-link fence
that separated the site from the cows' field next door.
Months' worth of sweat and work, hand-shifted earth and
sand and stone was removed in an hour. When it was done
and the farmer and machine had gone away, what was
exposed was flat scraped earth of rich chocolate brown.

This brown earth, now feeling the sunshine for the
first time in three-and-a-half thousand years, was a
Bronze Age field surface. It wouldn't bask there for long,
because below lay the Neolithic remains Graeme and
Hazel wanted to reach.

But Bronze Age people had farmed right here, because
they knew this patch was fertile, albeit stony and prone
to sand-blow. It was fertile because it had been laid over
Neolithic midden: the dumps of house-sweepings and
shells, dung and ash. Bone-heaps where dogs roamed,
looking for scraps.

By the Bronze Age the Neolithic houses were already
buried, mere stones sticking up through the earth, mere
annoyances.

This is what I meant about time contracting and expanding and turning round on itself. I had to remind myself of just how many centuries separated the two Ages, although only a few centimetres of earth.

Bronze Age, Neolithic. 'They're just labels,' said the archaeologists. 'People just got on with it. And besides, though we talk about the Bronze Age, very few bronze artefacts have yet been discovered on Orkney.'

'Look at this stone,' said Emily. She was working in a Neolithic house, or a structure of some sort, and was patiently excavating the skeleton of a small deer which lay on a slab within the house, for reasons unknown. But she stood to show me one of the stones of her struc-ture. Its upper surface was scratched all over, and its edge was dinked where the ploughshare had passed over it, stone on stone. Maybe the ploughshare broke. How they must have cursed, in their lost language. Dug out the offending stones, their forebears' walls and furni-ture, heaved them aside.

Eventually people quit trying to haul crops out of these small, difficult fields. The climate had cooled, sand blew in too often. They moved elsewhere, and in due course sand dunes formed, the same dunes that remained into our own times, till new winds rose and obliterated them.

But where did the people go once they quit the settle-ment at Links? Gone was the wild or unclaimed land of two thousand years before. They couldn't just sail off and found a new place, as their long-ago forebears had done.

'Not far away,' said Emily. 'You see that grassy mound along the shore there? That's an Iron Age settlement.'

After lunch, taken in the shelter of the site hut, Anna and Dan and I were sent back to work on the newly exposed area. We had to trowel through the field surface to reach any structures beneath. It was hard work. Dan is strong and could quickly tear with his trowel through the packed brown earth. He was nearest the wall.

He dressed always in black, a black scarf round his tied back hair, slightly piratical, and he wore a big bead on a leather thong at his throat. Anna, who was slightly built, worked in the middle and then came me, the newbie. We moved backwards, side by side, kneeling on pads, and, because the earth was thin, the enclosing wall began to emerge, what was left of it. As Graeme had predicted, more structures duly appeared within the settlement it defined, maybe houses, which they would have to excavate in the couple of months left of the season.

Despite being confirmed in their hunch, Hazel and Graeme looked weary. They had a very modern problem in the midst of the Neolithic: they were coming to the end of their funding. HES – Historic Environment Scotland – had repeatedly warned that this year would have to be the last.

An hour later I caught Hazel at her makeshift desk inside the shipping container, and I asked her about the funding. The nearer the deadline drew, the more features were being found; how typical. The budget of HES was not something the Neolithic farmers had given thought to when they built and kept rebuilding.

'If HES really pull out, what will happen?'

'We'll have to look elsewhere and make all sorts of promises. We can't look to the EU any more. There are other finding bodies, but...'

'What sort of promises?'

'Usually, to engage with people not usually engaged with archaeology. That kind of thing.'

Outside there was the sea and sand, the same lobster boat in the distance that came by almost every day, some gannets diving. Inland, some farms on the hill, a turbine, cattle grazing quietly.

'What people?'

'The kind of people who don't usually pee in a sand dune. Seriously, if we were to raise money by opening the site to the public, to visitors, to parties from cruise ships, we'd need toilets. There's not a metre of land here suitable for toilets that hasn't got archaeology under it. And I don't know if I want to be responsible for bringing cruise ships here...'

'What a strange thing to have to pander to, cruise ships. If the oil price jacks up – no cruise ships.'

You don't have to be an archaeologist to know the oil age won't last half as long as the Neolithic did.

Hazel went on. 'An alternative is to run it as a field school, with inexperienced diggers, but the effort of managing them, keeping them safe ... Having people "engaged" takes more time and energy than the actual work.'

'So. It just gets buried in the sand?'

'It won't be buried. That's the trouble. If it was all packed with sand again, it would be safe. But these structures are exposed now, so the wind will soon destroy them.'

Does this matter, is the question. Do we want to know how it was to be human, here, five thousand years ago? Do we want to know where we're coming from as we cruise into the future? What we were, or might be again? How we 'engaged,' if that's the word, how we configured our relationship with the rest of the natural world, with the planet.

Back on site, the conversation turned cheerfully cataclysmic. Dan, Anna and I kneeled in our row, scraped away the Bronze Age soil, and talked about climate change, about the global forces and corporations we feel powerless to resist.

We spoke about an oil rig which had broken loose in a storm and run aground on Lewis, how it was still sat there weeks later, still leaking oil.

Dan said, 'All it would take is one almighty meteor strike. One huge volcanic eruption, and we'd be back in the Stone Age.'

'It looks alright,' I said, flippantly. 'The Stone Age. Snug wee houses, sea views. Beef and oysters. Some weird ceremonial stuff now and again. A short life, but a life...'

'But we'd know how to do it! Your average Joe wouldn't. Your average Joe in the city.'

Dan plugged himself back into his iPod and worked on. He had the enclosure wall to deal with and, in its lee, many flints. His patch was covered in little polythene bags, each containing a bit of flint. Anna and I, just a metre further into the enclosure, had only brown earth which yielded occasional small morsels of bone. I pretended outrage when Hazel came by. 'Miss! It's not fair! He's getting all these finds, and we're not.'

Hazel's answer seemed visionary. She glanced and said, 'They must have been sitting on the wall, flint-knapping.'

Sat right there on their village wall in the afternoon sunshine, working and chatting. I almost saw them.

The next day, Graeme was more chipper. It was the end of the week, and things were coming together. The JCB had gone, the enclosure wall was found, there were indeed newly discovered structures within it.

'Now,' he said. 'We'll have to excavate them. That's our job. Dig into them and scoop 'em out. And then we'll run for the hills.'

* * *

Friday night was pub night. The island's only hotel has a small plain public bar with a jukebox and WiFi. We fell into two tribes: Westray farmers at the bar, in overalls and workboots; half a dozen archaeologists in their corner, scrubbed up nicely in clean T-shirts, sat on seats and banquettes. The two tribes were not unfriendly, not unknown to each other after so many seasons, just different. There were the archaeologists, all from elsewhere, who lived shifting lives of much travel, and there were farmers who had remained largely on their ancestral lands, often for generations.

Some of the archaeologists were already having to think about their next job, their next temporary home, and had laptops and tablets open as they filled in application forms and funding bids.

In due course, though, the laptops were folded away and Criostoir put money in the jukebox and pub-talk and stories came out, wisecracks and nonsense. Hazel and Graeme arrived and for some reason the talk turned to ghosts. It surprised me how many of these practical-minded folks were open to the idea of ghosts. No one scoffed. Maybe the open-mindedness and lack of dogma they have to maintain at work persisted into other aspects of life and death. And all that imagining the past. The Irish ones spoke of banshees. Criostoir said only people with clan names beginning Mac or O' could hear a banshee, and some still did, sure, the night before a death. Knockings and sounds.

But no one had heard of a Neolithic ghost, never a prehistoric presence, though they lived all day among their earthly remains. Ghosts have a half-life, it seems, lingering just a few hundred years, till they too fade away.

It was full moon or near enough, and I had to cycle over the island to reach the old house on the hill where I was staying. Dark roads between quiet fields, and fields of restless geese, and glimpses of moonlit sea. For the last mile the house was silhouetted against a moon-filled sky. Sandy and Willie were away that weekend. I was to be alone in the eight-times-blessed empty rooms, aside from one ghost-white cat.

Did the Links people believe in ghosts? They certainly needed their dead. Consider all the chambered cairns

Neolithic people built, with crawl-ways and low lintels, strange bone-houses concerned with the proper treatment of their ancestors. Cairns that fell out of use and out of memory, but lingered in the landscape to become the haunt of the fairy folk.

The weather changed during the night; I woke towards dawn and looked out the window to see rain slanting over the fields, over the old burial mound. By the garden walls around the house, the dog-rose bushes thrashed their white flowers.

* * *

The most famous find yet from Links of Noltland was discovered in 2009, not long after the dig began. That means she was late in the sequence, as they say. She came from a time more recent than they are working on now.

When the rain cleared, I went to the Westray Heritage Centre in Pierowall especially to see this find; she is on display there. The Heritage Centre is two conjoined rooms, recently built. The left-hand room is given to artefacts from the island's past, the right to some natural history, a mock-up of a sea-cliff with model birds, and some gifts and knitwear and books of local interest.

In the historical side, the Links of Noltland dig has a small section of its own. A video is played on a loop, with a slightly younger Hazel on camera, in explanatory mode. In the few years since the film was made, already much has changed.

I looked in the few glass cases, at bone pins for clothing, some flint and stone tools, the skull of a horned cow. Then came some Viking objects, bone combs. There was a straw-backed Orkney chair and some farming implements but I couldn't find the 'Westray Wife,' so I asked the attendant at his desk. His accent was from the Midlands of England, a place he had clearly left behind.

'Yes,' he said, 'lots of people miss her. She's in the glass case, right in the centre of the room.'

I'd missed her, because the 'Westray Wife' was tiny, a veritable Thumbelina.

I peered through the glass of the tall plinth to see a figurine formed of the island's reddish sandstone, only four centimetres high. Just an oval head on a blocky body, but that's all it takes to make a human figure. She has dots for eyes and one zigzag eyebrow, and scratches that suggest a nose but no mouth, but these features are hard to discern through glass.

On her torso are inscribed two circles which may suggest breasts, so giving her gender, but they sit high, nearer her collarbones. Her stone body is inscribed with fine lines, like those on the palm of your hand. They may or may not suggest clothing. She is not like the fat and funky Paleolithic 'Venus' figures that have been found across Europe; if anything, she is sweet and unassuming. She spent five thousand years buried among the rubble of a building, which had itself then been buried under half a metre of domestic refuse. 'Buried,' though, is possibly the wrong word. There's a suggestion that the figurine was placed in the rubble deliberately, to formally 'close' the building.

The 'Westray Wife' is the earliest representation we have of a human, in the UK, and she has become a motif for the site, almost a tourist attraction, if tourists can be drawn to a sandstone figure not four centimetres high on a faraway island.

Which they can. The attendant showed me a little booklet where they note visitor numbers to the Centre. The year following the arrival of the 'Westray Wife,' visitor numbers doubled. She is the island's oldest and most famous inhabitant. Whatever she was intended to do, five thousand years ago, she is potent again, in her glass box on a plinth, ancestral and watchful.

Three more figurines have since been discovered at Links, and others are now appearing on other Neolithic sites. One has come out of the dig at Ness of Brodgar on the Orkney mainland, and another, made of whalebone, has been rediscovered, after careful searching, in an old box in the store of Stromness museum. The whalebone figure was originally from Skara Brae.

As is so often the case, it's a matter of looking, of knowing what you're looking for.

None is as tiny as the 'Westray Wife,' with her curious zigzag eyebrow.

When the figurine was discovered, a researcher noted a similarity between her eye-dots under their brow and certain carvings on a lintel inside a chambered cairn on Papa Westray. There, similar eyes are carved on a stone in the deep dark.

Also in the Heritage Centre is the Neolithic Westray Stone. It's in a glass case on the floor of the foyer, as if they didn't know quite what to do with it. The stone is four foot long, eighteen inches high. A digger driver found it in the nearby quarry – or half of it. The stone had broken along its horizontal axis. This was around 1980. Archaeologists were called in and soon found the other half. The stone had come, they were sure, from a chambered cairn and had probably formed the lintel above the entrance passageway.

The thing is, the stone is carved with deep, trancey spirals, paired spirals, with spandrels in between. Raised high, maybe in a nightclub, with the right sort of lighting, it would be powerful and unsettling.

Eyes and spirals.

* * *

The sun was out again. I strolled along the road. After the rain, the calm and huge skies, the pouring daylight, the birds and seals. The community garden held splashes of colour in sheltered nooks, nasturtiums, Livingstone daisies. I met Criostoir, the big lad with his rolling gait. 'The weekends,' he said. 'So feckin borin'.'

'You need to come to the store,' said Graeme. 'At the weekend come to the store. Come to our house, and we'll take you.'

Graeme and Hazel live in an old schoolhouse in the middle of the island with their son and Hazel's elderly father. The classroom is still attached to the house. They were in their garden, lifting tatties, as I arrived, but the tatties had a species of blight. There was Hazel, a small Irish woman with a basket of blighted potatoes, a reminder of how marginal it all could be, this farming life.

The old classroom is a large bleak rectangle. They have plans for its restoration, but for now the ceiling is falling in. Graeme pointed out how the windows were deliberately set too high to let the schoolchildren see out. No gazing at their island and their cattle and their seashores and their homes. What they got was reading, writing, arithmetic, and a fair dose of the Bible, until the bell rang. Small wonder they sailed for Australia.

There was another shipping container in their grounds, and I half thought that might be the store they meant, so I was surprised when after our tea we piled into the site minibus and drove the four or five miles through Pierowall to Gill's Pier, where crabs and fish are sent off and freight is landed. From the pier head, Graeme and Hazel led me a few yards up a rough track. A warehouse to the left was packed with sacks of imported animal foodstuffs. On the seaward side, however, stood a dark Victorian behemoth in stone, three storeys high, with gables facing the shore. Three rows of six-pane windows did nothing to lighten its appearance; it was like a Victorian mill. On its high roof stood ranks and ranks of lums. Graeme made for the door.

I must have looked surprised and they laughed.

'What were you expecting?'

'Something the size of a garden shed, maybe. One of those nice old fishermen's huts in town.'

Graeme trundled aside the door and we entered into dust and gloom. Through filtered light from high windows, I saw plastic boxes stacked head high, and more boxes, and, through a partition, yet more. There were so many boxes that walkways had been created between them. Among the boxes, there were stones laid on pallets. But it was the smell that arrested me: the building held a pungent, musky mix of pitch, tarry rope, black-dark creosote, smoky things. Soot and fish. A wonderful low rich dark smell, a century old or more. It made me realise that the island is so wind-swept it is almost scentless.

Huge beams supported the roof, hewn from trees such as you can't find nowadays.

'It was intended as a fish-drying place. They hung the fish from the rafters and then walked up and down with wheelbarrows full of smoking embers. Didn't really work.'

'No...'

'But then, in just a few years steamships appeared and they could send the fish off quickly, so there was no need to preserve them. After that it was used for weaving, but that didn't work, either. All the looms and equipment went off to the Western Isles.'

Nothing left now but the smells. Such smells as are almost banished from the world, in a half-light, a barn-like light.

The three of us were surrounded by plastic boxes. Through a gap in a partition I could see yet more boxes. Ten years' worth, since the site began.

'There's more upstairs. It's the biggest Neolithic assemblage in the UK,' said Graeme. 'I don't think Historic Environment Scotland know what they have. They really don't know what they've got here. It's what would have come out of Skara Brae, if only they'd kept it. If people had recognised what they had back then. But here they have another chance...'

Both began moving through the stacks selecting boxes to open, taking out objects to show me. I held polished mace-heads, chunky beads of stained and polished bone, bone pins for holding clothing, scrapers made from sheep's knuckles.

Graeme opened one particular box to show me a slender implement reminiscent of those nibbed pens we used at school, to practise joined-up handwriting. It could have come from his own schoolhouse.

'You see how the tip is stained dark?' He said. 'We think it was used for tattooing.'

'Now look at this,' said Hazel. In a larger tub, laid on kitchen paper, lay a chunk of pottery two hand-spans wide, a broken fragment of what had been a sizeable pot. It had been incised with a deep and powerful spiral design.

'Where have you seen that design before?' asked Hazel.

'The Westray Stone, in the Heritage Centre...'

'... and in Ireland,' said Hazel, in her Dublin accent. 'The other place we are seeing these spirals is at the Bend of the Boyne, at Newgrange and Aboyne. You know that huge lintel stone there, at the tomb? We're beginning to think the peoples here on Orkney came

from various different areas. This design may mark the
Links of Noltland people as different in identity from
other groups, who favoured geometric designs. This is
what we're thinking. That there were different groups
coming here from different places...'

Hazel and Graeme showed me more beads, some
made of animal teeth, and half-made beads, lots of
beads. Thick pins of bone, as long as your hand, presumably used for fastening clothing.

'But look – this pin is made of bone, it's from a
domestic animal, but see how it's been shaped to look
like antler? That's a puzzle. We have these references to
the wild...'

For a moment, out of the twenty-first-century plastic
boxes stacked in the gloomy Victorian store, there
emerged a vision of people clothed in animal hides,
bearing spiral-designed pots, with hair braided, hanging
with beads, people crazy about cattle, young people
prematurely old, as we would think now.

Different groups, with their different clothing and
accents, tools and designs arriving here. But very soon
after their arrival, there would be no one alive who could
remember the journey. Doubtless there were stories.
Origin stories. Contact with other people of the same
ilk, who spoke the same language, at other settlements.
Great ceremonial gatherings, informed by movements of
sun and moon, risings and settings, alignments of stones.
The midwinter sunrise shines down the passageway at
Newgrange, the midwinter sunset illuminates the inner
tomb at Maeshowe.

How did they know that, these kids of twenty or thirty years old, with their bone and stone tools?

Spirals.

You wonder what they did with that tattooing pen.

Stone and stone, bone and bone.

Not that there was nothing else, it's just that all the other materials had simply rotted away: the soft hides, the clothing, the basketry of grass or straw. But there were suggestions of colour, minute traces of reds and greens on beads, even on walls, a sort of paint. There are frequent finds on site of ochre and haematite, which yield pigments of yellows and rust-reds.

* * *

I was almost glad when we stepped outside again into the fresh air and Graeme rumbled the door closed. Accumulations make me anxious. What to do with it all? The boxes and boxes all stacked up, all yet to be catalogued, dealt with, written about, kept safe. The sheer cultural responsibility.

Properly speaking it all belongs to the State – that is, to us the people, to the nation – but what does the State know about some plastic boxes filled with beads and bones in a Victorian store behind the pier on a faraway island, the stuff of five thousand years ago?

'There's enough here for thirty PhDs on bone alone,' said Graeme. 'Decades' worth of work.'

'I'd like to open some sort of centre here,' said Hazel.

They seemed remarkably sanguine about it all.

The tide was way out as we drove away. In Gill's Bay, the weedy shore was picked over by curlew and redshank. Out on the yellow sands, I saw a man with a metal detector. He was swaying the machine back and forth, as if it were some agricultural tool, maybe a scythe.

I said, 'That bloke's looking for treasure.'

Treasure, and you have the greatest Neolithic assemblage not a mile away.

Hazel turned back in her seat. 'The richest Viking graves ever found, pagan graves, were discovered here in Pierowall. They're under the council scheme now.'

Later, in the twilight of my room, I lay on the bed. It was a lovely room, with lace mats under glass tabletops, embroidered samplers on the walls, and an old spinning wheel set as a decorative feature in what had been the fireplace. Three tall windows, a mahogany chest of drawers. A refined, ladylike room well removed from the daily wrestle with the earth.

I lay there and went over in my mind the objects and artefacts I'd been shown, had held in my hands. Bone pins, figurines. Then, I wondered which I would choose, if God forbid I had to, to send into outer space in hopes some other intelligence would find it, identify it, and know it as a marker and statement of our species. What would I load onto the Voyager spacecraft? A bead? A polished stone axe?

I suppose it would be one of the ugly, grunting-looking stone ploughshares, as long as my forearm and twice as thick. It spoke of hard labour, not of decoration. The breaking of the earth. Of what we still call the 'daily grind.' It spoke to the 'Neolithic package' that revolutionised the world. Yes, I'd send that. It could hurtle through space like a meteorite, in hope that it might make landfall on some new shore.

'Was your world once wild?' a distant intelligence might ask.

Yes, we'd say. Till it went under our ploughs and the hooves of our cattle. Under the weight of our stuff.

* * *

There is a chambered cairn that quietly overlooks the site. A green hump on the hill. You could see it from the houses here, and they, the dead, could oversee you.

It seemed to belong to farmland west of the site, where the land rises.

Through binoculars I could see it was damaged. A single large stone was jutting out. Had it an entrance passageway, buried under the mound? A spiral-incised stone? A solar alignment? It had been got at by Victorian antiquarians, opened like an egg from the top, but no report survives. It had never been excavated since. I'd resolved to go up for a look and, that evening, after the others had left site, I happened to be passing just as the farmer was lowering himself from his tractor, two spaniels leaping after him.

His was the common arrangement, a modern bungalow adjacent to more ancient buildings. There was a row of low byres with repaired flagstone roofs that may have been houses once, and were full of straw and farm machinery now.

The farmer, burly in a blue boiler suit, had the strong slow accent of the island, rich like beef or cream.

'Would you mind,' I said, 'if I went up there and saw the chambered cairn?'

I asked just out of courtesy, neighbourliness, and because no one misses anything here.

'You could go,' he said, 'but there's kye up there. And a bull!'

'Maybe I'll not, then.'

'I wadnae advise it. They'll be there a good few weeks yet, maybe into October.'

The door behind him opened and his wife looked out quickly, to see who he was talking to.

'There's no much to see. But a few years ago a wumman came and she spent near the whole day sitting up there. I don't know what she was doing.'

'Getting into the mystic?'

'Aye, maybe that!'

Being a bit frightened of kye, I walked up onto the hill as far as I dared, to a field gate, and then farther up a rough slope, until the route between me and the cairn was blocked by the typical Orkney confection of barbed wire and stone strainers and bits of driftwood tangled in. It was not something one could leap in a hurry. Beyond the fence, four pale bullocks were already clambering to their feet, yellow tags in their ears. I wouldn't be the woman sitting there all day, not with this lot nosing and trampling.

I turned to go down again. 'There's nothing much to see,' the farmer had said, and maybe not. But it depends whether you are looking at the cairn, or from it. I'd wanted to see the view from it.

And here it was, the view from the dead-house, and it was stunning. On this bright day, from this hillside you could see for ever, overlooking the settlement on the Links below, and then the whole island beyond, its scattered farms and turbines, bays and cliff and sea to the northern horizon, and over to the island of Papay, which has its own Neolithic houses and cairns. You had line of sight to the little house called Knap of Howar, reckoned the oldest standing house in northern Europe. You would command miles, being dead, and the living could glance up at you from their fields, feel your presence, your authority, legitimising their place on the land. 'Yes,' you could say, as an elder might to a teenager setting out into the world. 'You've left the wild behind, you're doing fine. You're doing great, this is your land.'

I went home to my room, over the island, past fields of cattle and of barley. Pipits and wagtails flew up from the road. I entered the house, then opened the door to my room. The room was flashing. The calm, carefully furnished room was crazy with a silent pulsing light-and-dark. I stumbled back out into the gloom of the hall. Then I went back in. It was still there: the room was flashing fast enough to make me feel sweaty, druggy, glad I wasn't prone to seizures.

It was the sun lowering behind the turning vanes of the wind turbine. Just chance. It could only happen

right now, this minute. A few minutes more and the sun
would be too low in the sky. A couple more days and
the sun would have tracked southward, toward its halt
at winter solstice, when it would shine down the long
passage of the tomb at Maeshowe. Then it would start
edging back north. So just for a few days, maybe twice
a year, it would sink into the Atlantic exactly behind
the turbine, exactly in line with this window. For a few
days, twice a year, at this point in the evening, if there
was a wind, the spinning vanes would slice the sunlight
sent into this room and fill it with a frenzied rhythmic
flashing.

Our Neolithic friends would have loved it. Pity I
couldn't invite them round.

* * *

'The farmers. The island folk, the cattle farmers – they
must be really interested in what you're finding here,' I
said to Hazel the next day, when we were back on the site,
but to my surprise she shook her head.

'They're interested, but not connected. It's only the
Vikings they're interested in. It's the Vikings the Orkney
and Shetland islanders identify with. They're not British,
not Scottish, but Norse. Not prehistoric, Viking.

'We have well-wishers, but incomers are more
interested than the locals. Not in every case, but by
and large. Someone actually complained about the
archaeology "cluttering up" their Heritage Centre.'

'But the Vikings are so recent, relatively.'

'The Vikings "won",' said Hazel, with a shrug. 'If we had some names, that would help.'

'Prehistoric names?'

'Place names or personal names. That would help.'

The very names of the Orkney islands are Norse. The '-oy' or '-ay' suffix is Norse for 'island.' Eday, Stronsay, Westray, Shapinsay – all Norse, all a mere twelve hundred years old.

Criostoir leaned back from his patch of earth and declared, 'Sure – I don't understand this interest in the feckin' Vikings. And the Romans – the English are obsessed with the Romans. The Normans in Ireland. All conquerors. What's wrong with the people who were here first?' He gestured across the site. '*These* are your ancestors!'

'What do you mean, the Vikings "won"?' I asked, reluctantly, thinking of the ancient burial mound I could see from my window, which the Vikings had chosen to use as a fishing station.

'Just that. After the Vikings arrived, all traces of the older culture ceased. That's what the archaeology is suggesting.'

* * *

The site continued according to its own rhythm. Round and down, intense work in cramped spaces. For all we were outdoors all day, there was little exercise involved and it could be cold cramped work even in August. The waves drove ashore, the lobster boat toured the bay. From time to time bigger ships with strange superstructures moved along the horizon. But every day brought enlivening moments and laughter. One day a BBC crew appeared, driving down to the beach in a big black Range Rover. Everyone kept their heads down and pretended to be very busy as Hazel did the required. She showed the presenter Neil Oliver some prize finds, such as a polished Bronze Age pendant, but the producer wanted a retake. 'Can you emote more?' she asked Hazel. Then they went away.

Anna, my fellow digger, kindly invited me for a meal at the house she was sharing with Dan and Emily and Dawn. A good Italian cook, she managed to produce an excellent meal for us all of chicken and couscous. It was dark when I left; by then the others were sprawled on their orange sofas watching some old Quentin Tarantino film on Netflix. They looked like the seals hauled out on the weedy shore. If seals could watch Netflix, they would.

* * *

Near the quarry, now disused, where they found the spiral-carved stone, there are a few new buildings, intended for offices and light industry. One had become a pop-up cafe by day and a youth club by night, a community venture like so much else on the island. The teenagers have a big screen, computer games, fizzy drinks. It's theirs in the evening, but by day it's open to all.

I went in one day for coffee and home-made cake and fell into conversation with the lady who oversees things. Shy teenagers do the serving. She stood behind the counter. A woman in her late sixties, maybe. She told me she had been born a stone's throw away, on a croft of the kind that had remained until not long after the Second World War. That was when the horses went off, the tractors came on.

'We had a small croft,' she said. 'We had four cows, and hens. A lot of hens.'

'What was it like?'

'Hah, we had to boil tatties for their feed, chap it up with the oats – then we put light in – whether they laid better or not I don't know. There was aye work. There was thinning neeps. I didn't like that. But when you look back on it ... you didn't know any different.' She paused. 'My mother didn't keep good health.'

'Did you have electricity?'

'We had small engines.'

'Generators? Must have been noisy.'

'And a tilly lamp. A gas light!' She laughed, paused. 'I must be gettin auld ... We were never bored, we come home from school and changed our clothes, for you only had one set ... we got on with it.'

She paused again, looking around. 'It can't go on like this...'

'What do you mean?'

'Everything on your doorstep. The kids come home, it's phones, TV...' She paused again. 'There was something aboot a tilly lamp, it was warm...'

Again that pause, as though images were crowding back to her mind.

'No so many small crofts on the island now. When a small farm comes up for sale, a bigger one buys it, they dinnae survive.'

And paused again.

'It mightna be lang till Westray is just aboot a couple o ferms...'

'A big cattle ranch?'

'So ... I'm no sure what'll happen ... Kirkwall is too accessible, you can go anytime. We nivver did that. We just went away on the County Show day, or that. That was exciting!'

Pause.

'We just worked away.'

My coffee arrived in a cafetière. I tapped the WiFi code into my laptop.

'Would you go back to those days?' I asked.

'No,' she said firmly. 'I would not.'

We all know it. We can't go on like this, but we wouldn't go back either, to the stone ploughshare and the early death. Maybe that's why the folk here don't embrace their Neolithic site much. It's still too close to the knuckle.

The cafe lady turned to her tasks and I to the Internet. According to Facebook, font of all truth, Scotland had that day generated all the electricity it needed from renewables. Just enough for one windy summer's day, still.

Also that the world had used up its ration of resources for the year, and it was only August.

Also, according to the BBC local news website, the world's biggest tidal turbine was undergoing its final tests here on Orkney. It had been towed to Orkney from its manufactory at Harland and Wolff's, Belfast.

Also that the oil rig, being towed the other way, still sat where it had run aground on Lewis, still leaking oil.

From Shetland, too, news about tidal energy. The company concerned were 'absolutely delighted to be the first company in the world to deploy a fully operational tidal array, and deliver electricity to the grid.'

* * *

It was late August. My time on Westray was drawing to a close, but before I left there was a visit I hoped to make, to a young couple Hazel had told me about. Hazel had said: 'If you want to know about cattle farming, you should meet Nina and Jason Wilson at Noltland Farm. Just go to the door. They're South African. They make the cheese.' The small herd of cows which grazed a mere slingshot from the Neolithic site belonged to Nina and Jason. The cows were Ayrshires: creamy-coloured with archipelagos of brown marks on their flanks.

I did want to know about cattle farming, because it seemed a living link to the Neolithic. The whole island did. In almost every hillside field were cattle. Grazing or kneeling or looking over dykes as you passed, with yellow tags in their ears. Great bulls the colour of honey.

I knocked at the farmhouse door and was welcomed in by Nina, who was pretty and instantly likeable, with curly hair springing from under her woollen hat. She shut her five dogs away and took me through to their kitchen, and we sat at the table next to the Aga while Jason, tall and lean, came in from his fields. It was Jason who gave me the couple's story. ('He could talk for Africa,' whispered Nina.) They had been on Westray for only five or six years, though Jason had come to the UK back when Mandela was still in prison and the sanctions regime made it illegal for him to work here. He was even thrown in jail himself. But organic farming was what he wanted to do. A long apprenticeship followed, in flat English fields of broccoli. He met Nina. Nina had a background in film and film studies.

She caught my look. The nearest cinema was an hour and a half away by ferry; it showed the latest blockbusters.

'I know! I'd like to set up a film club here...'

Back then, they had never heard of Orkney. Then came a chance meeting with an Orcadian, journeys north, explorations, and a saga of failed bids, or blessings in disguise.

'And we got Noltland.'

The couple moved in one day and, the next, ploughed up the ryegrass to plant a species-rich herbal lay, with thirty varieties of grass. They've since seen a great increase in insects and wormcasts.

'What do your neighbours think?' I asked.

Jason smiled. 'Orcadians would never swap. I don't demonise conventional farmers. I mean, who's ruining the planet? I start my car in the morning. Farmers are not the enemy, they're good guys, they're not bombing anyone, they're trying to feed people. A good stockman loves his animals.'

'But they must look over your dyke and think that's interesting?'

'Oh, everyone is intensely interested in everyone else's farm!' laughed Nina. Now they have a herd of twenty-three dairy cows.

'And have they names?' I asked.

'Of course!'

'And personalities?'

'They're as different as human beings,' said Jason.

'And a bull?'

'Eric. He's called Eric. We share him with another farm. Lots of bulls are called Eric here. I think it's a Viking thing.'

'Would you like to meet them?' asked Nina.

Of course I would. Of course I wanted to meet the cows that grazed the same land as did the Neolithic animals so long ago, at Noltland, the 'grassy dunes of the land of cattle.'

They led me outside through the yard and a series of gates. Jason, long-legged in wellies, loped delightedly toward his cows in their field.

'Don't you feel a connection with the Neolithic folk?' I asked. 'They were right here...'

'Of course,' Jason replied. 'Their days were the same – summer days like this. They'd have been thinking the same things.'

'Such as?'

'I'm thinking about walls now, about protection...'

When the cows saw Jason and Nina, they all ambled over, nudging and shoving until the couple were standing in a crowd. Not me, though. I was a stranger and the cows were wary of me.

Jason scratched their backs while Nina gave me their names: 'This is Greta, a proper little madam. This is AC/DC. That's Onsie, she's a bit goofy. That's Butterfly, because of her ears. That's Buttons. Annabel. Daisy.'

Eric had done the required. All the cows were pregnant.

Theirs is the only dairy herd on the island. 'Time was,' said Nina, 'when every croft had a cow. But the 1983 pasteurisation act put an end to it. People sold their cows, their churns, forgot about it.'

The couple make an artisan cheese they call 'Westray Wife.' A little picture of the Neolithic figurine features on their labels.

'You got the brand!'

'No one else was racing for it.'

Amid the cows, we were looking inland at the island's shallow valley. Their view was of a gloomy castle, and, beyond it, the small loch, then farms on the hills, sheep on the peaty summits, the climbing road, the chambered cairn, two or three small whirring turbines under the huge island sky.

I said, 'When the Neolithic people brought their cows ashore here, the first ones, all this land would have been wild. Can you imagine? I wonder what grew here then.'

'I love this valley,' said Nina. 'Its different colours. Brown in the spring, then green. The cattle. Quiet, then noisy with tractors.'

'I see it differently through your eyes.'

'They were like us,' Jason insisted. 'Caring about their animals.'

Some folk say time is a spiral, that what goes around comes around, that events remote to one other can wheel back into proximity. Leaving Nina and Jason I walked down to the shore, feeling like a child again, glad of heart to know there is still room in the world for a summer's day and a cow called Daisy.

The sea was calm. No one else was on the beach, only some birds and two seals watching me from a few yards out in the water. I stood at the water's edge and sang the seals a song about time and change, and the seals, out of courtesy, listened.

Links of Noltland

II

In mid-October, almost two months after I'd left, I returned to Westray, sailing out of Kirkwall as slashes of orange light grew in the east and gulls flew over the still-dark sea.

On the island there was little to announce autumn, there being no trees. But all the fields were cut, and some held flocks of golden plovers. There were no swallows now. The cattle were all still outdoors, it had been so mild.

This time I was staying at the same hostel as the archaeologists, because a room was free. From there I walked through Pierowall and passed the school now filled with children, then Nina and Jason's farm, greeting their cows in their field, then turned down to the bay where the waves still crashed ashore. The cairn was on the hill, the wind turbine spun. I was happy to go through the steel gate, to see the barrows and spoil heaps, and greet everyone again.

A reduced team had worked on into the autumn. I recognised Hazel and Graeme, Anna and Maeve, Dan, Criostoir and Emily, all by their clothing. Emily's fluorescent waterproof trousers, Dan in his piratical black bandana, Anna by her blue woollen headband. They were still there, and counting the days till they left. All had now spent long months on the island away from their homes, always in each other's company. Backs ached and wrists were numb. Clothes were trashed. All jokes had been told, all yarns recounted.

'To be honest wit' you,' said Dan, setting down his wheelbarrow, 'I've left the site already. My head is already gone, it's just my body that's here.'

'You're home in Kerry?'

'With my dogs. Long walks with my dogs. The fella that's looking after them says they're fat. And I'm planning on buying a big TV.'

The site had been due to close at the end of September, but they had been granted a month's reprieve. Now, with weather in their favour, they were excavating up to the last moment. The final task would be to photograph everything, and then on the very last day cover the whole site with sheets of black plastic weighted against storms by stones and tyres and more stones. The selfsame stones as had formed successive Neolithic walls and hearths, now heaped aside, would be pressed into service again.

The team had been spared the massive job of burying the site completely under tons of sand, because HES had announced they wanted to come and laser-scan the whole lot before that happened. Laser-scanning would require weeks of good weather; it would have to wait till next year. Hazel and Graeme had received instructions to cover the site lightly, so it could be reopened again with relative ease.

'So, if it's open again,' Hazel said, sotto voce, as if HES might hear, two hundred miles away in their offices in Edinburgh, 'we might as well dig it.'

Criostoir kicked an earth-fast stone. 'There's stuff to be discovered under all this yet. To be sure. There's years more work here.'

The light had diminished since the summer. By mid-afternoon it would be cold.

Emily and Criostoir were working on a house with a substantial hearth. Emily had discovered, tucked into the lower right corner of the hearth, a stone chest the size of a shoebox, with a lid. No one had seen the like before. What could it have been? A warming place? A tiny bake-oven? A place for keepsakes dug into the hearth when the house had fallen out of use? It proved to be empty. Another mystery.

There were more prosaic intrigues, too. No one is sure how the houses were roofed. Driftwood, maybe. It was plentiful in those far-off days before Europeans discovered North America and felled its forests and dammed its rivers. Huge logs would have journeyed all the way across the Atlantic, to roll ashore here. Who knows what our Neolithic forebears made of them, what they thought their provenance might be. But they'd have been a boon.

The house which Emily and Criostoir were now excavating had lain under the Bronze Age fields. Back in August I'd helped Dan and Anna, now both deployed on other tasks, as they scraped away that covering of soil to reach the Neolithic remains beneath. It was as the directors had expected: within the confines of the enclosure wall, another early house had begun to emerge with sundry other structures, as yet undiagnosed.

Across the site, Maeve still inhabited the same house as she had been working on before. Lean and funny, a runner, she had spent months in its tight confines, turning round and down, round and down: she knew it intimately. Now it was almost done. Hunched in her worn green waterproofs, she had several days of planning to do and was anxious to complete the job.

'There's something about a site closing down,' she said. 'An atmosphere.'

Maeve was spending her days leaning over a grid of string, with a plum bob in her hand, marking on graph paper the exact relationship of stones and gaps she saw on the ground. At 1:20 scale, a work of beauty and exactitude was emerging, which helped her see the site more clearly than the real thing.

'You see, I hadn't really spotted this line of uprights until I drew them ... and these doorways. Look at that!'

What she had discovered since August was a well-made entranceway in her house, which pleased her because it was aligned exactly with the entrance to the house opposite. Someone creeping down the passageway would be presented with a door on the left and a door on the right. Two people emerging at once from their respective houses would have bumped heads.

The exactitude was part of mounting evidence that the Neolithic village had been planned, in an architectural sense, and well built. It had been thought about, possibly even drawn – without paper, of course – before work on it began. But prior to the planned village there had already been two or three houses. This was Graeme's thinking. Two or three houses of which Emily and Criostoir's was one.

The site was closing down, but over and again people said the excavation was not the half of it, it was the meticulous 'post-ex' where the real work was done. The cleaning of bones, the examination of flints and grains. All the boxes piled in the Victorian store down at the pier would have to be opened, sorted through. This was what people were beginning to think about. Some were planning to return to Westray to begin this indoor work, after a winter at home. Maeve put her head in her hands and pretended to weep: she was one of those who'd come back to help analyse the animal bone, boxes and boxes of it. 'I could still be here into my forties!' she wailed.

'How old are you now?'

'Twenty-nine! But I'm sure I saw a cat-bone. That'll be interesting, to get a proper look at that. I'm sure it wasn't a pine marten or a wildcat...'

'There weren't supposed to be any cats.'

'Not until the Iron Age. But I'm sure it was a cat ... And the deer. One of the research questions is whether the deer were wild or farmed, or semi-farmed. These are the things we'll discover post-ex, hopefully.'

Anna was there, she was frustrated and, she said, 'a little bit heartbroken' to have to leave, though her joints were aching, because her area was just starting to look interesting. She was squeezed between the enclosure wall and a house wall; a well-made drain defined her area. The drain, a little stone-lined trench capped with stone, ran from somewhere in the centre of the site toward the enclosure wall in a manner which, in Emily's word, *respected* the curve of her house wall, suggesting to Emily that her house was there first. Anna said, 'My hunch is that it was a different area of use; there are bones and flints, decorated pots. Maybe it was a dump!'

She was going to see her family in Romania, and then? She shrugged, sadly. 'I don't know.' She was entering into the strange shapeless world of post-PhD blues. A sense of life and career not quite getting started, at an age when many of the Neolithic folk would already be elders, if not dead.

The days had certainly shortened. At lunchtime on my second day, I walked around the site while the others were in the shipping container. It was too cold to sit outside now. The site lay silent in the low sun, which brought out the reddish and yellowish tinge to the sandstone that formed the enclosure wall. The marram grass of the dunes stirred, and all was quiet except for the twittering of a small flock of snow buntings. They had just arrived, chased out of the Arctic by the darkening days. Only five of them, a little family, they flitted around the edge of the Neolithic houses, pecking at dried seedheads.

By mid-afternoon the sun was low enough to send shadows across the site, and every crumb of trowelled earth became sharply visible, each with its own minuscule shadow. The low light made fine work difficult, slanting in at the corner of the eye.

'I think, in the end,' said Emily, 'that this was all just like a shanty town, then they moved off altogether.'

* * *

The season turned on a dime. That night I stood outdoors under the Milky Way. Occasional shooting stars flared, and I heard sounds of restless geese down at the lochside. A few farmlights prinked low on the land. But by morning the wind had changed, bringing cold squalls of rain in across the sea. You could see them coming, grey ghosts out of the north-west. Even the snow buntings had moved on.

The team worked, heads down and hoods up, as rain slanted in across the site until suddenly Criostoir raised himself upright in his shredded waterproofs, in his filthy jeans and boots, and spoke for all.

'Feck it. Let's go home.'

Links of Noltland

III

It's surely a fine, well-chosen day when you drag your
boats ashore, with the bound and terrified cattle, the
sheep under nets, the seed corn and tools and overexcited
children. An island shore you must have known and
reconnoitred. Perhaps there's an advance party here
already, who've put up shelters. What was your name for
this place? Where did you say you were going, when you
set off across the water? From where? Not far, surely. A
creeping north rather than a leap into the unknown.

You build a low encircling wall, stone on stone. Within
the wall shelter your first houses, with driftwood pillars
to hold up the roofs. You make beds of reeds and skins,
tend the fires that will reek for centuries in the dark
interiors. You turn the cattle out the gate into the scrubby
woods, set the bairns to watch them and sing them back
at night, within the wall. Outside rise heaps of ashes and

bones and broken pots and all those household sweepings
and scraps, dogs sleep there curled up warm. But what
of the wall? Maybe it's a sense of wildness that makes
you edgy, as it does us now. The wall suggests your
status, sets you apart.

You come stooping out of your doorways, wearing skins
fastened by bone pins; you pierce your skin, braid your
hair, heap yourselves with beads. You cut down trees,
burn the logs that roll up on the shore from who knows
where. You plant barley, though you haven't quite quit
foraging: a bit of hunting here, a bit of fishing there, an
arrow and a net – but it's the cattle you adore, those
warm beasts with big horns, benign but wild, with soft
breath and eyes and soft skins. Cattle you butcher with
stone knives.

You suffer painful joints and toothache. You die in
childbirth, lose children to infections. You cough and
cough. Despite that, generations pass, the Links becomes
home, the place you return to after visits, festivals. A
marriage partner might arrive from another village,
another island, she might make a few changes, but
you're here. The place is yours because the ancestors say
so, from their ossuary on the hill.

Buildings fall out of use, are reclaimed and altered and,
fair enough, across seven hundred years, why wouldn't
fashions change? Maybe there are stories and songs of a
heroic past and origin, already long out of mind.

You know how to work with fire and stone, clay and
skin, grasses and herbs. You know butchery and
stitching. You stroll the beach seeking wood and flint and
seaweed. Bone – you are experts on bone. You make and
fire rough pots; some with your signature spiral design.
You like to sit on the wall in the sun and work flints into
blades, enjoying the midsummer light.

Beads, tools, every made thing, is the work of your own
hands; you have strong hands. You instruct the children in
these crafts. Teach them what to love and what to fear.

Everyone is known to everyone, and everyone works:
pain-ridden elders, simpletons, small children confined
within the wall, all are given simple tasks. There is no
shortage of tasks!

You know the stars in the winter dark, the green aurora
borealis, the solstice moment of rebirth. Midsummer
gloamings when you can ramble outdoors at midnight,
enjoying the light on the sea. The birds' movements are
known to you, swallows and snow buntings, geese you
can catch with a net. The voles that creep in and eat
your grain – they were stowaways – you brought them
with you unawares!

There are festivals and great gatherings – spectacles of
stone and fire, solar and lunar shafts of light, movements
across land and water – but it's hard to leave the fields
and animals, as any farmer will tell you still.

One day you leave. You don't go far. The place falls into ruin, then the sands blow in as they'd long threatened to do. Who was it who crept back to the ruined village, entered a house there and left a small stone box tucked within a hearth, before the houses were buried completely? What was her name?

Time is a spiral. What goes around comes around. The box is found again, but only after five thousand years have turned. By now we number in our billions, have built mega-cities with instant global communications, and send spacecraft out to explore unknown shores. We can live to be eighty, ninety, a hundred years old! You early farmers were a success beyond measure. But millions shrink in poverty. Others build high walls and fabricate missiles. Sea levels rise, storm winds are bearing down on us. We are becoming ashamed of our own layer – plastic and waste.

Of course, we open the box, hoping for a token, a keepsake, even a message of some kind, but there is nothing inside.

The Inevitable Pagoda

THE DAYS ARE LENGTHENING. In the fields around town, the stubble has been ploughed back into the earth and soon the fields will be sown again, obliged to yield again. But for now the earth has a breathing space, it lies open to sun and moon, bare, rich and brown.

The farmer has left scarce a margin, scarce room for a mouse to run. Head down, you walk this margin as best you can, the wire fence at your right. Every few paces, you reach into the ploughed earth and pick up some new fragment of crockery.

In no time at all, you have a handful.

A spiral in three shades of blue, against a background of sapphire blue.

A faint lacy pattern, like frost on a window.

Faraway skies, where it's raining blue rain.

A chunk of earthenware, creamy yellow glaze all crazed now.

Diamond shapes, packed together like cells seen through a microscope, each blue diamond with a dot at the centre.

Fronds, like ferns or pondweed, branching tracts, blue-grey.

A swag of tiny bellflower shapes, maybe lily-of-the-valley.

An inch of saucer-rim, butter yellow.

A built structure, surely part of a pagoda? With a blue branch. Yes, the inevitable pagoda.

A slipware bottle rim, sandy brown.

A cup handle, partial. One green brushstroke, enough to suggest a leaf.

You spit on them and wipe the spit with your thumb. Not one is much bigger than an eye, a blue eye, or a postage stamp.

A no-nonsense chunk of earthenware, glazed conker-brown. Hand-thrown, somewhere nearby.

Heaped in your hands they suggest cottages and parlours or farmhouse kitchens. Rooms with scrubbed stone tiles and dressers showing off Willow pattern plates. Farmers and cottagers. Folk who fetched water from a well in an earthenware jug, or fed their hens from an old plate. Some pieces are handmade of the local clay, some factory made and dainty, but none is throwaway – each must have been washed a thousand times, which was women's work. A wedding gift of dishes. 'It starts when you sink in his arms...'

Remember your grandmother's formal front room, her ornaments, the plates on the wall.

Dropped by accident, thrown in temper, perhaps grieved over – they all ended up on the midden and were eventually ploughed into the field along with the dung, where they remain, sometimes to resurface for a while.

Now you have a handful, spanning centuries. And there's another piece, winking from the ground; this could become obsessive. Each is a glimpse of a life and a time. It begins to sound like a clamour rising like mist from the empty field. All the stories, the voices, the dead...

You look out over the new-ploughed acres as over human history, and the next field too and the next, and all the fields...

Ach.

They fill your hands, these fragments, these stories, but with a wide gesture, you cast them back across the field again.

Surfacing

You're losing their voices. When did that happen?
You're forgetting the sound of your mother's voice, and
your grandmother's. They died within eighteen months
of each other a decade ago and today you realise you
can't quite bring their voices to mind.

You make an effort, and recall a story. Not a story,
they were neither of them storytellers. They placed no
value on that. But you recall Nana telling you about her
father being brought to the surface after a blast below
ground. He'd been laid off, maybe it was during the
Depression, and in his time idle he'd lost the sixth sense
which warned miners if something wasn't right. He'd
only been back at work a few days before he was caught
in a blast and brought to the surface with a sheet laid
over him with holes cut for his eyes. He was sent to a
convent hospital, where the nuns often tended injured
miners. A Protestant, he would never again hear a word
against nuns.

Are you making this up? How could you? But
you can't recall the sound of the telling. Something

remains, however: the cadence. You recall the less patient cadence of your mother. She seemed to expect you to know and understand things without them ever having been explained. Nana's speech was lower, her accent richer with the Scots she'd never regarded as an impediment to progress, because she was never going anywhere.

'Brought to the surface' is the recurrent phrase. There is a desperate list of mining accidents in Ayrshire, as in every coalfield. Fatal ones, that is. The many non-fatal injuries went unrecorded. Blasts were not so common, more frequent were crushings caused by roof-falls or runaway wagons and hutches. Like the time a shift of miners was being hauled up an incline to the surface in wagons, four men to a wagon, but the chain snapped. Or the Knockshinnoch Disaster of 1950, when a new working broached the bed of a glacial lake, causing countless tons of peat and sludge to empty into the tunnels deep below, filling the escape routes, leaving 129 men trapped down there. Thirteen were lost for good, but the others were there for three days, until fellow miners rescued them by cutting through from old disused workings nearby, which were gas-filled. They were all led to the surface wearing breathing apparatus.

Nana's voice is coming back, it was just mislaid. You hear her short phrases and pet words. She often sounded a bit bewildered. The world was complicated, puzzling. Then there was the time of terrible silence, when she forgot how to speak at all, when for weeks or months,

God it felt like years, she sat straight-backed and mute, trapped in the black mine of depression. It was during the school summer holidays, she'd been brought to stay with you. One morning Mum sent you three kids to McColl's for sweeties and so you skipped off. Sweeties! First thing in the morning! But it was a ruse. You realised that when you turned the corner home and saw the ambulance, the neighbours watching and the crew bringing her out, covered by a sheet.

You must be misremembering. Why covered? She was overdosed on sleeping pills, not dead.

Dead to the world. She had ECT, to shock her to the surface of her own mind. She was to be hauled through tunnels up and out of that place, for a while at least.

Once, she told you about having diphtheria as a small child. Her throat was closing, the spent air unable to reach the surface, the new air couldn't enter. Her father was preparing to cut her trachea. How did she know that, did she overhear, despite her fever? And with what would he operate? Doubtless his own razor, called a 'cut-throat' for a reason. But it didn't happen; the crisis must have passed, maybe a doctor arrived with a better idea. And where did they put her, to isolate her and her infection in that crowded house? You can't reach her now to ask.

The deep mines are all closed, the pithead buildings cleared. Some efforts are being made to heal the wounded land by planting trees, and blocking drains to restore the moor, so the curlews might return. Bings and old railway beds are grassing over. The open-cast scars are deep gouges that might one day become lochs, maybe. Sometime deep in the future.

Once, in Nana's tenement flat that smelled of town gas and coal (her voice comes to you), she caught sight of herself unexpectedly in the mirror that hung above the mantelpiece.

'Oh, I look like ma mither!'

'What was she like, your mother?'

A pause, as if puzzled, as if she had forgotten. As if no one had ever asked, which they hadn't. Why should they? What was her mother but a miner's wife, a mother of seven.

'Ma mither was very kind.'

From the Window

THE WINDOW OVERLOOKS a neglected back green where a few shrubs grow with their backs to the wall. Under the washing lines, grasses heavy with seedheads all incline slightly southward, and among the grasses a lone yellow plant, maybe a ragwort.

It's evening. From time to time the grasses move in the breeze. Now a feather comes wafting down, a pigeon's or a herring gull's. It's cloud-grey, as though plucked from a cloud.

A century-old back green, walled in on three sides by tenements four storeys high and stacked with other folks' windows, other folks' lives, their ages and stages, their phone wires and drainpipes, slate roofs and all the disused lums above the roofs near-silhouetted against a sky that's glowing white between greyish clouds. The opalescent northern sky: it is late summer.

You're watching the grasses move, and the way the telephone cables serving the flats radiate from a common pole, planted out there in the back green, and how the wires divide the air into segments. You're watching the chimneys darken and that cool sky as it intensifies in the last light, a cold glow. Just looking out the window.

That near-white sky. Hadn't you seen the same shine and tone earlier in the day? Yes, it was the pendant your daughter was wearing, an oval stone set in a silver rim, on a silver chain, the stone just the size of a thumbnail. A pendant she often wore, cool and calm, that changed in the light between cream and pale grey.

You'd been shopping, and had bought some kitchenware for the life she was about to embark on as a student in another city. You noticed the pendant against the neck of her terracotta-coloured top the moment before she turned away. Shopping done, she was off to meet friends, leaving you standing on the street in late midlife holding a bag containing a colander and two tea towels. 'You can take these for me, Mum. Bye!'

Put it another way: for a long moment the sky above the ranks of disused chimneys was the hue of a polished stone worn by a young woman as she walked away up the street into her own life. You watch her go – long hair, skinny jeans – thinking, what?

Thinking: may she be spared.

Thinking: okay, what now?

You go home. The evening is your own. Having put the colander and tea towels in her room along with her other new things, bedsheets and plates, you spend a long moment looking out of the window as the light changes, thinking: okay, then, what now?

A Tibetan Dog

FAR AWAY FROM HERE, in the province of Amdo in China, there lies a town called Xiahe. To the Tibetans, Amdo being a Tibetan province, the place is known as Labrang. It is the site of an important monastery.

A river flows through the town, which eventually joins with many others that rise on the Tibetan plateau to become the Yellow River. The Yellow River is three thousand miles long and is nowadays dammed in a dozen places and poisoned by industry.

In Xiahe this river is spanned by a concrete bridge. On the south side of the bridge stands a hugger-mugger of Tibetan dwellings with flat roofs; on the north runs the town's dusty main road.

One evening many years ago, walking alone, I was about to cross that bridge from the Tibetan side when, emboldened by dusk, a little terrier came rushing out and nipped my calf. I didn't see it coming; the first I knew was the sensation: 'nip' is the very word. I felt a quick pain, so spun round to see the creature already scarpering back among the houses, even as I yelled. I think I threw a stone. The brute had rushed out specially to bite me, a foreigner. The tiny wound was dribbling blood, so back at the hotel I dabbed at it with iodine.

I had two companions there: Sean, with whom I was travelling, and Elena, a young Italian woman who was staying down the corridor.

'Look,' I said. 'A dog bit me. A Tibetan one.'

They didn't seem too bothered.

'They love dogs, the Tibetans,' said Elena. 'They say they are the reincarnations of lamas who ... how do you say?'

'Didn't make the grade?' said Sean.

'Lama or no, the damn thing bit me.'

And then the incident was forgotten. Of course it was. I was not much older than my own children are now. I had my travelling adventure, came home, a quarter-century passed. Partners were met and children were born and grew. Friendships were forged and lost. Jobs, projects, homes, bereavements, the stuff of life – if we're spared. The undammed rush of life.

If we're spared.

* * *

As you may know, having biopsies done can be horrible. The tests themselves are awful: hospitals and long needles, shock and bruises, but then comes the waiting and the fear.

In my case, it was a week between the tests and the results. I already knew my lump was a cancer, but there were questions about how aggressive the cancer was, and how far it might have spread, and what treatments might be offered.

What are we meant to do, to feel, at these volatile times? Each to her own. We try on and discard different attitudes to see if they fit and none do, then leave them lying around to kick at, like a teenager her clothes. Grief and grace. Bewilderment. A pious gratitude for the life we've had and a struggle to remain composed and then the rage: why the actual fuck should I remain composed? Then, calm. Why feel anything? It's all in the lap of the gods.

One night during that fitful week I managed to sleep some, and had a vivid dream. In the dream I was walking along a busy street when suddenly I felt a hard pinch on my left calf. Twisting round, I saw a small dog in the act of biting my leg. The dog waited till it made eye contact with me and only then, when it was sure I had seen it clearly, did it unclamp its jaws, release me, turn and trot away.

What a strange dream! I woke with it clear in my mind, the bite, the dog's look. But something had changed in me. I woke relieved and strangely reassured that I wouldn't die of this cancer, not this time, not now. I was being nipped, and would be released.

And that dog! It was the same Tibetan mutt, utterly forgotten until now, twenty-five years later. The dream-nip was the very sensation I felt then, in the same place. How funny, to think my subconscious must have waited till I'd fallen asleep, then gone rummaging through a million long-lost memories to find an image it could craft into a message I would wake from and understand. And what had it come up with, so triumphantly? That little dog, and its teeth.

Now that it's all over, it pleases me to imagine that the lama-dog knew what it was doing back in 1989, that it was laying down an act of kindness, and that I'd regret the stone-throwing and cast a blessing after its memory instead. I'd thank it for becoming that dream-metaphor trawled up to reassure me in an hour of need.

The dog is long dead now and quite gone, unless it is indeed caught in the eternal wheel of rebirths, in which case I wish it a happy incarnation, next time round.

Anyway, strange dreams for strange times. My husband came with me to the hospital to hear the results of the biopsies and, because it was June and mild, we waited in an odd little courtyard with a lone thin tree before being called in. The surgeon and the nurse explained that the prognosis was good. They offered a plan, an operation, more tests, and assurances: we could hope for a happy outcome.

Soon, I broke the vow I made to myself at the time: to live for the day, to relish every moment of being alive, to smell the roses, all that. Time may work in mysterious ways but it still passes. However, although life gathered pace again, one thing lingered at the back of my mind. The Tibetan dog dream had opened a hinterland of other memories. It had reawakened the experience of being in that Tibetan town, at that time. A time of being young. Memories had surfaced because of the dream, and I knew I wanted to explore them with calm hindsight, to remember and maybe write about them, when the chance arose.

* * *

As it happened, it took ages before I could settle to the task – even the cancer was becoming a distant memory – but the idea persisted and eventually I cleared my desk and cleared my mind as much as possible, the better to immerse myself and remember the town of Xiahe, and my few weeks there when I was half as old as now.

First, though, I needed to find the notebook I'd kept at the time. That wasn't difficult, just a matter of squeezing through the tiny door that opens from our attic room into the space under the eaves, a dark cubbyhole where the temperature drops. In there, next to the Christmas decorations and an old Olivetti typewriter, is a cardboard box full of my old notebooks. A lot of them! Mostly they're abandoned when there are still more blank pages than filled. A new direction of thought, a new adventure, requires a new notebook – or so I tell myself.

I rummaged down through the layers of my own life, as stored in the notebooks. Some were spiral-bound, good for opening flat on the knee. Some were small enough to slip into a back pocket, most were slim enough to bend. None was fancy, no colours or gimmicks. I knew the book I was seeking was unusually thick and business-like; I remember reasoning that I'd be abroad a while and replacements might be hard to find. Then it was in my hand, a robust black Alwych thing with blue edges. It was easy to identify because at some point on its travels I'd pasted a postcard on the cover showing a Tibetan Buddhist painting, a *thanka*. Seeing the card again, I dimly remembered buying it at a street stall, not knowing what it meant, just liking the exoticism of the image.

The old notebook retrieved, I closed the box, shoved it back into its place in the dark, reversed out of the cubby-hole, fastened the half-size door. I had my handwritten notes, and also – in another box – some evocative black-and-white photographs taken by my travelling companion at the time: street scenes, portraits.

Then they were on my desk with their curled corners and thumbed edges, real things from a time before the digital age. Archaic objects with material existence in the world. Photographs, developed by hand in a darkroom. The handwritten notebook with its picture postcard on the front. Museum pieces, but they seemed like old friends, which they were, for what is a photograph or a notebook? A reaching out to a future self, the future self of next week or half a lifetime. I was the utterly unimag-ined future person the notes had been made for, although I didn't know it back then.

The card shows Shakyamuni, with blue hair and long earlobes, sitting enrobed on a stylised lotus flower, almost floating above many fiery demons. Amid calm yet sumptuous shades of blue and orange, he represents perfected wisdom, all-compassion. The Buddha on the front cover and, when I opened it, the notebook released a particular faint smell: paper, of course, maybe ballpoint ink, but also a herby, dusty aroma. Yes, of course: I'd picked some wildflowers at the shore of Qinghai Lake and pressed them between its pages. They were still there, flower-ghosts, fit to crumble at the slightest touch.

* * *

To compose the piece took several weeks. Absorbed, I was able to carry the 'feel' of those days through my present tasks, inhabiting two worlds at once, as writers often do. The notes were scarcely adequate, just earnest jottings in small handwriting, but it was the best I could do at that early, bewildered age. I was twenty-seven, a young woman trying to be a writer, trying to find a way to live that life, whatever that life was. Are we supposed to feel something when we encounter our younger selves? Nostalgia? I felt no nostalgia. Are we supposed to feel something when told we have cancer? What? Says who?

It was late winter as I wrote, the sky darkening the window in the afternoons. What emerged were questions, to which I still have no answer.

I deliberately avoided the Internet, and its unnuanced, memory-crushing, what-actually-happened gobbets of 'information.' No dream-dogs there.

Perfected wisdom, all-compassion. I wonder where Elena is now.

The Wind Horse

BECAUSE THE DOOR to our room had dropped from its hinges, it would open only a hand-span, then rasp against the concrete floor, needing a hefty shove to open it completely. The rasping was a noise we'd come to know well, with our comings and goings.

The hotel was a grudging, recently built affair in the Chinese end of town, right opposite the police station. You entered the hotel from the main street, an unmetalled thoroughfare where umpteen bicycles trilled by, and small chugging tractors, and official-looking Jeeps bearing men in peaked caps. It was the only place in town foreigners could take a room, but even so the attendant was inclined to refuse. She was a young woman in her mid-twenties, much the same age as ourselves, who had her own small quarters behind a sliding glass panel in the lobby.

We insisted and entreated and at length were given the cards to fill in: name, passport, all that. Then we were allocated a plain room on the first floor, midway along the corridor at the back of the building. The hotel girl led the way with a bunch of keys. She always admitted us to the room in this manner. Every time we came back from our wanderings in the town or the surrounding hills, we had to summons the girl and her bunch of keys. She never smiled back, not at us anyway. She led the way along the grimy corridor, a small figure in slacks and a blouse and worn little shoes.

Always, the door stuck. Sean was six foot or so, and even if he leaned over the girl to shove the door, in a jokey way, she never smiled.

The room she led us to had been swept, but not recently painted. Bare greenish walls, two narrow beds with mattresses of horsehair or straw, a washstand and tin basin, a rickety table. On the table, a red Thermos flask with a cartoon panda printed on it. A dangling bulb above. Curtains hanging as though from a gibbet. It wasn't much but we were tired, dirty and thwarted, and relieved to be anywhere at all. At least there was a decent-sized window, a long rectangle that looked onto the backyard, an arena of grey gravel with a boiler house and latrines on the far side. Then, beyond a brick wall, the land fell a few yards to a shrunken river.

It was one of the tributaries of the Yellow River, and maybe in spring it ran with snow melt because hills surrounded the town and we were quite high, nine thousand feet or so. But it was very early June, the snow had retreated and the hills were green. Above the town grazed herds of sheep and yaks. We could see from the window mist lifting in the mornings and, on the nearest summit, a cairn with a bundle of prayer flags straining in the wind.

Prayer flags. I remember thinking we'd come a long way to see that: some tatters of cotton tied to a pole.

* * *

We'd arrived in Xiahe by bus, around three weeks after leaving London. I'd spent my mid-May birthday in Rawalpindi; from there we'd taken a mighty Bedford bus up the Karakoram Highway to Gilgit, where we spent a few days before making another arduous bus journey through Hunza and up over the Khunjerab Pass. These names are wonder-filled and exotic to me now, elevated with a sense of altitude, of jagged snow-plastered mountains, blue skies and strikingly cold air.

I recall a high valley with a river running through it, austere and beautiful, and villages like glowing gems spilling down barren mountainsides. I recall sitting on a cold riverside stone, nursing a headache as we waited for clearance at the border post, at fourteen thousand feet, before the long descent toward Kashgar. There the people were mostly Uighur. In public many women wore full-face brownish veils. There were jugglers and acrobats outside the mosque, and yoghurt was sold on the street in shallow dishes. The yoghurt was cool and thick.

In Kashgar, we learned from some Americans that Tibet was resolutely closed. There were protests and clampdowns, not only in Tibet but in Chinese cities too, strikes and unrest. The Chinese authorities were expelling from Lhasa any foreigners already there, and forbidding others to enter.

We faced a dilemma. Should we return to Pakistan and wait there, maybe in Hunza or Gilgit town, hoping for the situation to ease? Or press on, and see what happened. We pressed on, crossing the Taklamakan Desert, a three-day journey over grey bleak gravel. From the bus windows we saw abandoned dwellings and sacks and sacks of dark sand, gathered by god knows whom, awaiting collection that never came. At every desolate oasis town, we heard the same news: 'Tibet closed,' 'No foreigners allowed.' In the town of Golmud, we joined the milling throng at the bus station, a press of bodies. There was a sign on the wall in English: 'Travel to Autonomous Region is forbid to foreigners. Martial law is executing in Lhasa.'

Executing in Lhasa. We tried nonetheless, mouthing our request through a little wooden hatch. The ticket-seller slammed the hatch shut.

Also on the walls were messages scratched like hobo marks, some in English: 'For Lhasa, try southern truck stop, not here.' 'Sam – we are heading east. J & T.' At the southern truck stop, no driver would give Westerners a lift, and fair enough. We trailed away, not wanting anyone to get into trouble on our behalf. As we left the truck stop a Tibetan monk in maroon robes sitting on an upturned box offered us a wan smile.

And now we were in Xiahe, a place Sean had suggested because the town was ethnically and culturally Tibetan. It had grown around of one of the largest Tibetan Buddhist monasteries, the ancient Labrang Monastery. But the town lay in eastern Amdo province, which was deemed

to fall outwith the designated 'Autonomous Region' of
Tibet. Though Tibetan, Xiahe was, in effect, in China.

Another bone-shaking bus left Lanzhou and wound
uphill for several hours into air cool and clear after
the heat and city dirt. When we descended from the
bus, it was into yet another yard of gravel and puddles
surrounded by shacks. But this time, even before I'd
shouldered my rucksack, a grey-haired old woman
approached me. She was wrapped in a thick sheepskin
chuba, with beads at her ears and throat, a flash of gold
in her teeth. She took my hand in both of hers, nodding
and smiling and speaking to me with sentiments I could
only guess at, as I nodded and smiled in return.

* * *

I was glad our room was at the back. From the front
there rose a constant ballyhoo of construction works
and bicycle bells. Even inside, it was noisy, with a daily
clanking of buckets and gruff shouts, and there always
seemed to be someone hawking up phlegm with a sound
like cloth being sheared. Every day brought the swish of
the hotel girl's broom as she swept up cigarette butts and
the husks of sunflower seeds. Sometimes another young
woman came to visit her, bringing a baby, and the two
of them played with the baby, in its little red knitted
trousers. But mostly she worked alone.

And there was the police station, directly opposite,
secure behind its walls and metal gates. On its gateposts,
posters showed grainy images of hapless men. I presumed

they were 'Wanted' posters. Without language, spoken or written, we were as babies ourselves.

There was noise but also song. Each day workmen came to the hotel yard to sieve heaps of gravel and load the fine stones onto a handcart. It looked a desolate job but sometimes they sang shanties. There was also a Chinese song, maybe it was traditional, maybe it was the current number one, because we often heard it wafting out of windows from radios or whistled on the street. It was just a simple melody, a woman singing in a high girlish voice. I grew to like it, in a wistful way. We had our own Western music, too. Sean had brought a dozen cassette tapes and a Sony Walkman, so we could have reggae or The Doors, again; 'The End' played as though on a loop.

There were other guests in the hotel. One was a tall monk who wore brown robes and tied his hair in a topknot. He may have been a Taoist, he may have been Japanese, I don't know, and I regret that I didn't try to speak with him. From our window we could watch him make his way to the boiler house every morning, almost gliding in his long robes. Every time, he would pause to bow to the labourers, who'd halt their work for a moment, nonplussed. If you encountered him, he bowed from the waist. He was gone again after a few days, on his perambulations. Another guest was a young woman also about our own age, whom we'd remarked on. She had thick black hair and dark eyes and she wore heavy dark woollen clothes. She kept a puppy, which she somehow managed to smuggle into and out of her room, the last room on our floor, at the front.

After a couple of days we coincided in the corridor, the terrier squirming in her arms. She greeted me in Italian-accented English.

'Oh,' I said. 'I thought you were Tibetan!'

I must have said the right thing, because she was obviously pleased and exclaimed 'Why?' as though it hadn't been deliberate. As usual, she was wearing local clothes, a little cross-over jacket with brocade around the hem, black cuffed trousers. A turquoise ring. Her black hair drawn back into a bun or plait. She smelled of woodsmoke, incense. She chewed gum.

'No, I am from Milan.'

'But you speak Chinese. The only time that poor hotel girl smiles is when you speak to her. Doesn't she mind about the dog?' I asked.

'No, she is nice, really. It is difficult for her.'

'And you speak Italian, of course,' I went on.

'And English and Tibetan!'

'You speak Tibetan?'

'I have spent two years there, in Lhasa. You have seen Lhasa?'

'No ... we were trying to get there, but...'

'Ah, the sky! This Lhasa sky is like nowhere else in the world. But I was thrown out, pah! But I am still here. Amdo is Tibet, whatever this Chinese government says. Lhasa! It's true they are destroying and destroying, but...'

'But..?'

'Only when we have been heartbroken can we be truly happy.'

That was the first we knew of Elena.

Sean had arrived by then, lugging his tripod. Here was someone he could talk to about Lhasa's blue skies, the wanton destruction, places he'd visited and longed to see again. The Potala Palace, monasteries, tearooms they both knew.

Later Elena invited us into her room. It was plain, of course, one windowpane was broken and had been mended with brown paper, but she had made an effort with it, as if she intended to stay, by fixing her own drawings to the walls, and a little printed mandala or Tibetan calendar, and by burning incense. The musky scent lingered in the room as it did on her person. She had a few books and a teapot – and the dog, of course. Aside from the puppy, her only indulgence seemed to be chewing gum.

She said, 'And now we have this demonstration in Beijing!'

The cities were closing down, strikebound. This is what we were hearing. There were strikes and protests in the cities we had so recently passed through, but we had seen nothing of them. Students were demonstrating, especially in Beijing, and, of course, the Tibetans were in open revolt, hence the military law 'executing in Lhasa.'

The next day another room became occupied, one on Elena's side of the corridor between ours and hers. Three Czech men arrived. Together they were so bulky they barely fitted into the spartan space they shared, but most of the bulk was Marek's. He was the ebullient one, a mountaineer like Sean and a self-styled businessman. He was a sort of tour leader or guide to the others, because he spoke a bit of English and seemed ballsy. He wore denim jeans and a loose leather jacket.

'We speak English, too,' we told Marek. 'Not much use round here. We've no idea what's going on.'

Of the other two, Zenek was a photographer, again like Sean. He was fine-boned, more sensitive and observant, communicating to us and Elena with gestures, smiles, long looks. Sean and he shared the international language of cameras and lenses.

'Me expeditions, he exhibitions!' said Marek.

The third man was called Alois. He was older, maybe fifty. He wore baggy cargo trousers and shirt and a sort of fisherman's waistcoat with many pockets, because, incredibly, he was a butterfly collector.

'A *what?*'

'Yes, he will collect butterflies!'

'You mean, with a net? In a Buddhist town?'

The Czechs confirmed the rumours we had been hearing. The cities they had passed through to reach Xiahe were indeed now strikebound, with train and bus networks at a standstill.

'Xining is closed!' cried Marek. 'Lanzhou! Chengdu! The government will fall!'

Sweetly, and quietly, three other guests had also arrived and been shown to a room in the basement. The Taoist monk had wandered on his way, and in his stead had arrived three Chinese art students – very young, two boys and a pretty girl who wove her hair in two sticking-out plaits like a doll. The boys wore

denim and had grown their own hair long, in peaceable
defiance, like Western students of the 1960s. The taller
of the two wore a bandana round his head. They smiled
often, and carried ink and sketchbooks when they went
around town.

The Czech men were on holiday.

'Holidays in China?'

'It is because we are from Czechoslovakia. We may go
nowhere, only China and Russia. *And we HATE Russia!*'

* * *

From the hotel we made forays out into the town.
Between the eastern end, with the hotel, police station
and Chinese businesses, and the western end, where
lay the monastery and Tibetan quarter, there ran three-
quarters of a mile of open-fronted shops and stalls.
Bicycles rattled by, Flying Pigeon brand. Jeeps and small
tractors. The shops and services were all up a few wooden
steps. There were dark and fragrant kiosks of tea and
spice, apricots, walnuts, knives and hardware. There must
have been a cinema somewhere; it was advertised by a
board with pictures of pretty film stars. The road followed
the river, though the river was treated as little more than
a sewer behind the hastily thrown-up buildings.

We walked up this main street almost every day; there
was always something new to see. A Muslim shopkeeper
wearing a white skullcap, totting up on an abacus, a
leopardskin hanging from a peg, for sale. A book-binder's,
with rolls of paper huge as tree trunks.

We often went to the monastery, which was called Labrang. Its enclave filled the lower end of a side valley, like a walled village in itself, far enough from the town to be peaceful. The main buildings were whitewashed, with green tiled roofs with flying eaves. The monastery must have been the reason this town sprung up in the first place, as it was hundreds of years old. Its monks were of the Gelugpa order, the order to which the Dalai Lama belongs. Shaven-headed, they wore the mulberry-coloured robes and yellow hats that His Holiness has made familiar in the West. We'd often see these robed men and boys walking through the town or sitting in teahouses. On the first day I saw a dozen of them in a trailer drawn by a tractor, laughing, robes flapping, careering off out of town to heaven knows where. Maybe up into the hills. Beyond the monastery the road led to the high grasslands; we had the impression it petered out somewhere upstream. Up on those slopes lived families of nomad herders encamped at the summer grazings.

Very soon after we arrived, I think the first evening, we made our way to the monastery, walked clockwise around its precinct walls, then slipped in through an open gate. We found ourselves among high-walled lanes. The major buildings, the temples and colleges were three storeys tall, and blue cotton curtains above their windows rippled in the breeze. On their roofs, golden ornaments caught the late sun. I remember quietude, and a smell of woodsmoke or juniper-smoke.

We entered the courtyard of a temple. There seemed to be no one around, though we could hear wood being chopped with an axe, a closed gate. Sparrows chirped. Beneath a porch with decorated architraves was a heavy double door painted with subtle tiger stripes. Each door had a brass-hooped handle choked with prayer scarves. The door lay very slightly ajar. We dared to cross the yard, mount the wooden steps which were dipped with age, and creak the door open a little more, just enough to look inside. We beheld a mysterious womb-like otherworld, a hall that smelled of age and butter-lamps. Carved painted pillars held up a smoke-darkened painted ceiling, candles softly illuminated the faces and folded limbs of many gilded statues in niches at the wall, and glinted brassware, on the figures on painted *thangkas*.

Of course we wanted to explore the monastery, encounter the monks, take photographs, fall under the charm or influence of their services or rituals.

We'd come a very long way, and I think ours was a beguiled but well-meaning curiosity. We realised we had to be circumspect, respectful – it was a monastery, after all. But we'd heard rumours that the monks were under careful scrutiny, even that the monasteries had been infiltrated by spies. It was said that a deal had been struck with the Chinese government: if the monks wanted their monasteries to survive, then they would have to allow them to be treated as theme parks, opening the ancient wooden doors to noisy tourist groups by day. If they made this concession, they would be allowed to function normally at other hours. There were fewer monks than there used to be; not all was as it seemed. Who told me this? Sean, after his experience in Lhasa the year before? Certainly Elena.

Evening was the best time for the monastery, when red-tinted clouds drifted over the hills, and the roofs shone. If Sean and I went there – he shouldering his tripod – the monks neither welcomed us, nor sent us away. The lamas had a lot to put up with, but if we did meet one in the monastic precinct, he almost inevitably smiled and nodded to us, apparently not displeased to see Westerners, or so it seemed. But we were tourists too, wandering around, peeking in at the temples to see the *thangkas* – manifestations of psychological states deep and strange to our eyes.

Skirting the monastery, winding along at the foot of a green hill, was a paved path used by local people and pilgrims to circumambulate the sacred buildings. The path ended with a row of shining white stupas, what the Tibetans call *chortens*. The stupas were weighty structures, shaped somewhat like huge upturned handbells on a plinth, maybe fifteen feet high, white and bright. They radiated thin ropes, like guy ropes holding down a tent. Each rope was tied with small bells that tinkled in the breeze. Stray dogs gathered there, yellow-flanked creatures that ate scraps brought to them by kindly old women.

This area was where people gathered at the end of the summer day, strolling in a sort of Tibetan *passeggiata*. *Passeggiata* with added merit-building: after they'd laid their foreheads reverently on the base of the *chorten*, the people moved on to a long avenue of prayer wheels.

They often came in family groups. Some were obviously
hill-folk, by their attire: ancient chubas unfolded and
rolled around the waist, striped aprons for the women.
Their eyes were crinkled after years of sun and dung-
smoke, a glint of gold showed when they smiled. Felt
fedoras were popular, sometimes sunglasses. Pilgrims
arrived in town, dusty from the road, striding with staffs
and bundles.

The prayer wheels were cylinders painted with scripture in red and gold – there must have been dozens of
them, doubtless some auspicious number – and they
turned on greased pivots with a particular squeak and
clatter, the handles worn by countless hands. Everyone
spun them after his or her own fashion. Lusty young
herdsmen moved quickly down the line, turning each
as he might spin a girl at a dance. Grey-haired elders
nearing the end of their days moved slowly, often having
to arrange their walking sticks in one hand before
reaching with the other for the wheel, to build up a little
more merit in this incarnation, hopeful for the next.

One evening we heard a cymbal clashing. A lone
monk was up on the temple roof among the ornaments,
beating in rhythm. In response, lamas in heavy woollen
cloaks and yellow hats laid over their shoulders emerged
from cell doors around the courtyard and made their
way to temple. We stood aside, trying not to be noticed.
The monks began chanting as they gathered on the wide
threshold, removing their boots. It was the temple with
the subtle tiger-striped doors. When they were inside,
we sat quietly at the threshold, and watched as the

monks within the darkened interior sat cross-legged on cushions. A couple of latecomers threw themselves in, robes flapping, to take their place in the chant. Until this point, the chant was a low humming drone, but soon, like a beehive discovering speech, the sound began to take form, low and gravelly.

An elderly lama, wearing a heavy cloak and holding his yellow hat at his chest like a fan, paced up and down between the rows of seated monks, rather in the manner of an old-fashioned schoolmaster. He seemed to be leading the chant, pacing then turning, so the folds of his cloak swayed at the floor.

Sean and I were not alone at the door. A few more laypeople had arrived. A couple in Tibetan clothes prostrated themselves in reverence, then watched the ceremony, still lying down. A little boy of six or so, in a blue tracksuit. To my surprise, a young soldier in green uniform took a place. From the corner of my eye I saw the star at his shoulder begin to sway back and forth in time. I focused on the grain of the wood on the foot-worn doorstep.

The monks' rhythmic chant continued, then the tenor of the sound changed, the grain of the wood swam back to my awareness and I realised I'd been transported. How long had passed I didn't know, but some monks had begun leaving the hall, brushing past their motley audience to return a few moments later with pitchers full of a drink, milk maybe. Each monk produced a bowl from somewhere in his robes, which was filled. They all drank. And then it was over. The lamas emerged into the evening sunshine, pulled on their boots and were away.

There were moments of connection, too. One evening I was walking by the monastery when a boy monk called to me, a novice of ten or twelve, with a sweet manner. He was sitting on some steps poring over a slate of schoolwork. What luck! On his slate was the English alphabet, and lo, here was a native speaker strolling by. He beckoned me over. He was doing well, could recite the letters, but he was defeated by 'W.' He pointed to the 'W' on his slate, and made a helpless gesture. I sat beside him, and a small group of shaven-headed boys in robes gathered to watch and laugh as I drew the letter carefully in my own notebook, then passed the pen. 'Dubble-you,' I intoned. 'Dub-elle-you,' the lad replied. We went on with a short cheerful lesson. I saw him and his classmates several times after that. 'Dub-elle-you!' they'd call, waving across the street.

* * *

We spent our days wandering, looking, taking photographs in Sean's case. In the dusty town, in the surrounding hills, sometimes together, sometimes not.

The sky had a sense of altitude about it, there was a feel in the air. For all the seeming exoticism and meditative calm, there were obviously tensions and flashpoints. Rumour must have been rife, as this was a Tibetan town and Tibet proper was under martial law. Strikes and protests inflamed cities to the east.

But our small orbit was the street and back alleys, the Muslim quarter with its pagoda, the Labrang Monastery, the surrounding hills. Sometimes we saw the Czechs and joined up with them. We saw the art students too, who were always together, and we'd wave.

I liked to see the horses hitched to telegraph poles in town, waiting with hooves cocked as their owners played Space Invaders or ate ice cream. I admired the women from the back as they examined goods in a shop, in their long skirts, their hair arranged into 111 tiny plaits and finished with a horizontal band of turquoise stones. I could look and smile, but what did I learn of their lives, the prostrating Tibetan pilgrims, the stallholder deftly working an abacus, the ice-cream girl with her barrow, who sat with her chin in her hands when business was slack? Nothing at all.

There were plenty of dogs in town, and long-haired pigs that rooted in muddy alleyways, and one day in a wayside yard uphill from the main drag I encountered half a dozen yaks, black, horned, saddled with bamboo rings through their noses, and beside them sacks filled with cakes of their own dried dung. Often I wished I could draw, like the art students. I'd have drawn those yaks chewing the cud, their animal patience.

It became Elena's habit to call out down the echoey corridor with a sort of ululation, especially if she had news, gathered from her own sources. Her days were a mystery to us, but she was almost always in her room of an evening, with the little terrier. If we heard that whoop, we went. The strikes were spreading, the whole country. Something would give. The Czechs were jubilant.

* * *

One day, in the hotel, the art students asked a question that bothered me. We didn't socialise with the students, not on the street. Or, rather, they kept a distance. As with the monks, we had to be circumspect. They had to be careful. But there must have been a mutual curiosity. I was alone and the question was asked in the hotel corridor and delivered, for once, by the girl, in careful and polite English with Chinese accents. She said, 'Please, are you worker, or student?'

I couldn't answer. Were they the only options? The gravel-sievers, the hotel girl, the striking traindrivers in Xining, in Chengdu – they were workers. The novice lad with his 'W,' the young people standing in front of me, and those we'd heard were encamped in protest in the public square in Beijing. They were students.

But what were we? No wonder the hotel girl seemed sullen, putting up with unkempt foreigners who stood so much taller than she, who kept turning up, who had no language, who demanded rooms. What were they? Or the monks, seen as often in teahouses as in the monastery precincts – what were they?

The students all had flawless pale complexions, interested shy eyes.

'Worker or student?' I asked Sean later.

He was laid on his bed, in jeans and T-shirt, left arm over his eyes, playing Burning Spear through the tinny speakers. 'Tell 'em we are as lilies of the field,' he said.

I did once encounter some monks engaged in hard physical work. They were beside a path which wound up from the monastery out onto the grassy hills. First I heard a pounding, and turning a corner saw a dozen monks with arms raised, hurling heavy stones down between their feet. They were packing down the earth ready to make a new building. Others were working with spades and mattocks. They were all shaven-headed and, though labouring, wore heavy monastic robes, in shades from plum through crimson. It was the shape of their bare arms which made me realise they were not monks at all, but nuns, young women building – what? A convent?

Two male gaffers were directing operations, and a handsome older sister scolded the girls for halting in their labours to smile at me. I think they were all glad for the diversion. It was sunny, and shadows fell on their robes; their boots and hems were muddy. At that moment, a low door in an ochre-red wall opened and another nun emerged, stooping, carrying a tray of ash to dispose of, with three puppies gambolling at her feet.

There was another building site, too. One day, we came upon a part of the monastic enclave we had not discovered before, a courtyard outside a large assembly hall. Something was going on. Two white, official-looking vehicles were parked there and a small truck, and workmen moved among mounds of earth, mortar, wood and wood shavings.

The hall doors were wide open, and within we saw not candlelit statues, but brash electric arc-lights shining on a ladder or scaffold. Was there drilling, banging? That was the only time someone flapped at us, to make us go away. Monk or lay workman, I can't recall.

'Those posters slapped on the monastery walls, do you know what they say?' I asked Elena later. It was becoming a habit, to ask Elena later.

She shifted her gum.

'Huh. That the monastery has been taken over by the State for its protection. You know there was a fire?'

An electrical fire, perhaps not accidental. An excuse for the State to move in and make a show of repairing and caring.

* * *

On two or three occasions in town, during those days, we heard words dropped quietly at our ears. It might be in a busy teahouse or on a back lane, wherever people thought they couldn't be overheard. They were voices of tense young men who had a few words of English. 'Please, you know what's happening?' Or: 'Speak English? Have you BBC?' But, no we had no radio, no short wave; we knew less than they did about the strikes, or protests in Lhasa, or the student demonstrations in Beijing, eight hundred miles away. With a discreet word or a shake of the head, we had to disappoint these earnest people, who slipped away.

As for the other Westerners, we waved to each other in the street, met for a bowl of noodles. Sean often carried a camera, and cajoled people into posing for him. We never saw Elena, though. Where she went by day or whom she saw, we didn't know, though she said she knew people in town. In Lhasa, before she was thrown out, she'd got by with a little language teaching. Maybe she'd picked up a few students here, on the quiet. We never saw her eat. Did it occur to us she might be penniless?

One morning it rained hard. It often rained; the valley was prone to short-lived thunderstorms. We stayed indoors watching rain pock the gravel yard and fill its potholes. I was copying passages from a booklet I'd borrowed from Elena, a selection of karmas and sutras by the first Dalai Lama, recently translated into English. There were instructions on developing the Bodhi mind:

> *Visualise the sentient beings who have sufferings. Determine to free them from it. Think – May they be freed from suffering.*
>
> *Meditate on the beautiful mind of love. Visualise the sentient beings who are without happiness. Determine to place them in joy. Think – May they be happy.*

When the rain eased, we went to Elena's room and said, 'We're going for some noodles, will you come? Let us buy you lunch.' but she just smiled as though the thought of noodles amused her. 'Or let's go down to the monastery. There's a teahouse...'

'Ah, you like teahouses!'

'...beside the *chorten*. They do wonderful sweet tea with those round seeds in and you can watch the people spinning the prayer wheels.'

'I know it,' said Elena. 'Perhaps I will meet you there later. First I will make a visit, my friends will give me food. I have friends in this town.'

She rose and stood looking out of the window, in her black jacket. 'The girlfriend I am visiting, she has just come from prison. Making leaflets, you know?'

Then, as if it were an equivalent: 'After the rain, big yellow flowers are coming. This the people like.'

* * *

We did try to ask the young students about their lives and their art. They were shy, always smiling. Perhaps they were chary about being with us; trouble would follow if they were seen consorting with Westerners. Perhaps we intimidated them. The men especially were so much bigger, physically; Sean was tall and blond, Marak burly. But one day we all chanced to meet in the grimy hotel corridor, and we formed a huddle.

We tried to ask them about the student protests we were hearing of, on the streets of faraway Beijing. But these students were far from strident. The boy with the red bandana round his long hair spoke for them all, with Elena translating as best she could.

'He says, "We are not revolutionaries. Some reforms would be adequate."' The lad paused, then spoke again.

'He says, "Life is like breathing and breathing and never being able to exhale."

'He says, "We are looking for beauty, with our art. We are looking for flowers."

'He says, "We challenge the government with beauty. Not fighting. Not politics."'

'Do you understand?' Elena turned, looking directly at Marek.

Marek snorted.

The same boy showed us his sketchbook. Street scenes in red ink, a few broad lines, and look: a woman in a chuba, pulling a donkey on a rope, the donkey pulling a cart laden with brushwood. A nomad herdsman, with saddlebags slung over his shoulder. Here a poor stunted blossoming lilac tree I recognised, having passed it many times. Chinese students, on a sketching trip to the Tibetan town. Maybe they were exoticising the Tibetans, but weren't we all?

As I recall, Elena only once accepted an invitation to eat. She and I went to a noodle house that smelled of woodsmoke and was the domain of a stooped arthritic old lady dressed all in black – black jacket, black tight trousers, down to her tiny black socks and slippers – who moved by holding onto the rickety furniture. Although it was June, her teahouse always had a wintery fug; there was woodsmoke and cigarette smoke, and shafts of light falling through cracks in the walls, where steam swirled from pans and kettles. A hefty bowl of noodles cost pennies. We sat on benches alongside slurping workmen, a jar of communal chopsticks on the table.

'What will you do if they don't open it again? Lhasa, I mean.'

'I will wait. I have friends in this town.'

'Could you teach here?'

'No. I have some translation, for a very small publisher. English into Italian. You?'

'Take the slow train home to Europe, I suppose.'

It wasn't something I wanted to think about. The future. Worker or student? I had done with student. Worker held no appeal.

We ate, paid the old lady's more able assistant, ambled up the street together passing stalls selling knives and tobacco, a street dentist, a blind musician.

Bicycles jangled by. Near the bus-station yard, we met Sean and Marek and Zenek. They were obvious figures on the jostling pavement, big, tousled, blondish men.

Alois was up on the hills with his butterfly net.

Sean was laughing. 'We're all going to the barber's. Zenek says we've got to come and watch him having his head shaved.'

Zenek grinned at the mention of his name.

'What for?'

'Moral support?'

'No. I mean, why's he having his head shaved?'

'He wants to look like a Buddhist monk.'

Zenek rubbed his head with his hand, a rosary wound round his wrist. 'Buddhist good!' he said.

* * *

One day we climbed out of town by a worn path that followed a stream, a tributary of the unloved river that flowed through town. It was hard going, the town was at nine thousand feet – enough to begin to feel it. At length the flutter of the builders' tractors gave out and the path wound on past wayside cairns, climbed onto a green plateau, where the hills seemed to billow away forever. There were ruins up there, mud-walled monastic retreats the Chinese army had reputedly destroyed. The hills were in their summer blooming; soon the town seemed far away. Up on the hill bees droned, and larks rose twittering into blue silence. And there were butterflies! Black butterflies I immediately felt anxious for. Alois would be up here somewhere, pouncing with his net.

On high points of farther hills, prayer flags hung. In the distant flanks of the low hills roved herds of sheep and cattle. We met two women, just sitting on the grass, one older and wrinkly-eyed, one young. From among their layers of clothing, and with big smiles, they produced some dry and sandy bread, which they broke and offered us. We all sat, exchanging nods of misunderstanding and laughter. The bread was rock-hard and tasted of nothing, the women smelled of woodsmoke and animals. They had a pet calf with little flags in its ears, which nuzzled into their hands. Then they sang, a pure soulful sound which carried far in the clear air.

That night Elena called us, with her customary ululation, and we found her sitting cross-legged on her bed, wearing her black little jacket and trousers, cradling the dog, her papers scattered around her. She told us what she'd heard: that the strike had now spread to the whole country. That Beijing was completely closed. No foreigners could leave; only embassy staff, because they were being expelled.

'Why?'

'So they will not see!'

'See what, Elena?'

'Bombing the universities.'

Don't be ridiculous, I thought, but said nothing.

She went on, 'These art students, they are making friends with the Tibetan people. With the student demonstrations in Beijing, the Tibetans are kind to them. They are very nice students. They like the Tibetans.'

Then, with a little shrug, she said that she was being followed, but she seemed neither surprised nor outraged.

* * *

A travelling opera troupe arrived to stay in the hotel and, for one night only, transformed the place. The concrete, echoey acoustics suited their voices; a stringed instrument sounded from the basement, a woman sang a few notes outside our door, answered by a tenor elsewhere. Why speak when you can sing? All day they sang phrases to each other, and snatches of song. Even the cute little number one tune got the operatic treatment. Then they were gone, and it was back to the clanking buckets and spitting.

One evening, very soon after that, Sean and I were returning from the monastery. We'd been within the precinct and Sean had taken some photographs of a lone monk concentrating as he made a ritual design on the ground with a substance that may have been sand or flour. The monk had glanced up, Sean had made his 'May I?' and 'Do you mind?' gestures, and the monk looked down again to his task, non-committal.

Making our way back to the hotel we'd happened upon a bunch of kids playing football and joined in for a while, to everyone's mirth, and then it was dusk. We were in a residential warren, a lane with high walls where gates of family houses opened onto a lane. Suddenly a gate opened and a middle-aged man looked out. He checked the lane was empty, then he beckoned. Had he seen us coming? He was plainly dressed, in a Western-style shirt and trousers, there was no threat in his manner, only urgency – there was something he wanted us to see. Was he Tibetan, Chinese, Buddhist, Muslim, a worker, a scholar? We couldn't tell and it didn't matter.

We stepped quickly through the wooden gate, crossed a tiny yard into a room under a low roof, where a woman, doubtless his wife, was standing back with her hands clasped at her chest. There was time only for a glance around: red and yellow quilts folded on top of a chest, two chairs, a Thermos on a side table, a picture of a turquoise lake amid mountains, and a black-and-white portable TV. The TV was switched on; it showed a grainy, badly tuned picture. This was what the man wanted us to witness.

He pointed toward the screen and hissed, 'Beijing! Beijing!'

Through the grey fizz, we saw tanks, rolling. Tank after tank.

Then, abruptly, we were out again, onto the empty lane.

*   *   *

That evening or the next, Elena summoned us down the corridor. She must have waited, listening until she heard us arrive, the hotel girl leading with the keys, the door jarring on the floor, then waited a few more moments to allow the hotel girl to pad away downstairs again, before she let out her ululating cry. She was sitting cross-legged on her bed, her few books and a little box of drawing chalks scattered around her, incense burning at the window.

'Hiya!' I called out, but stopped short. Something in her face. 'What's happened?'

'They've killed four thousand students in Beijing.'

Into our long moment of silence she spoke again.

'It happened days ago. Only today did I hear. People running from Beijing are arriving. They could not get out of Beijing, for the shooting.'

Sean began pacing the tiny room, swearing and swearing. Then he sat down.

'Do the art students know?' he said.

'Yes. The Tibetans are embracing them. It is dangerous for them. The police want the student leaders. They are not student leaders, but...' Then Elena almost laughed. 'They think they can stop it this way!'

'Have you radio?' asked Marek later. 'Short wave?' Again we had to say no. We had only the Walkman, the reggae tapes and The Doors. 'Break on Through (To the Other Side).'

Soon the art students slipped away back to Xining or Chengdu or wherever they'd come from, the three of them in love with the world and each other, imaginative and brave, contesting the government by drawing flowers. 'They said the heart was gone,' said Elena.

Then: 'Elena – where's your dog?'

'I gave him away. Nice people. They will look after him.'

* * *

Life went on. There was to be a fair, a race day, a gala. Elena had said so and, sure enough, to announce it, a couple of days later twenty or so Tibetan horsemen cantered through town wearing high hats and smart boots, white shirts blousing out, red sashes. Behind the hooves' dust came policemen on bicycles.

It was nearing midsummer. On the appointed day people rode horses, walked, cycled upstream to a wide grassy glen a mile or two upriver, beyond the town. Some arrived on trailers drawn by tractors. The glen was enclosed by sharp, rough little hills; smudges of snow still lingered in the corries. Herding people had come down from the high grazings and erected windbreaks, white tents with blue circled designs, eternal knots in the corners. They lit fires and cooked meals, in huge cook-pots rested on stones. There were plenty of horses with tails tied, bells on their bridles, tethered to ropes

laid on the ground. A great deal of horsetalk was going on, that much we could understand. 'Chu-chu' is what people said to horses, as they approached: 'chu-chu.'

Old ladies tended the cook-pots and juniper fires. The smell was of woodsmoke and horses – and cordite, because there was a rifle range, gunfire echoing among the hills. Tinny music played. The men were in their best riding boots, the women in their finery, with braided hair, heavy earrings, beads. Someone unloaded a pool table from the back of a trailer. There was a tug-of-war. Gathered like this, come down from the hills, they must have learned about the protests and martial law and the clampdown and the killings. They must all have known.

The fair was presided over by a Living Buddha, a figure in yellow on a podium in a tent decorated with eternal knot symbols. The Living Buddha was flanked by two dignitaries. Girls wanted to present prayer scarves to the Rinpoche; we moved close enough to see what was going on. We watched one girl approach when she was summoned. She unwrapped her scarf from its paper, bowed three times and, holding the scarf out, began to sing. The crowd quietened as the girl sang against the volleys of gunshot from the rifle range, but her nerves got the better of her, she faltered, looked stricken, then dashed at the Rinpoche to present the scarf. Very soon after, the Rinpoche and his attendants left in a car, at speed. Some girls were still waiting to present their scarves; their expressions turned from excitement to disappointment.

I looked around for Elena. Why had the Rinpoche been hustled away at speed? Was he even a proper Rinpoche? Who were these dignitaries anyway, these minders? But Elena was nowhere to be found. In fact, we hadn't seen her at the horse fair at all. Maybe she had other business to attend to, back in town, more important than answering all our questions.

* * *

It was evening, a few days later. In the Czechs' room, the thin beds were pressed into service as sofas. We'd bought some beer and rigged up the Walkman with its tinny speakers. There was Elena, Sean, me, the Czechs – not much language in common. But we had The Doors, again. We played 'Take It As It Comes' and 'The End.'

Alois had found some caterpillars – they were alive and eating leaves in petri dishes on the windowsill. I don't know how I'd ever thought Elena was anything but Italian. For all her asceticism and Tibetan modes and her dark attire, she had a particular pout of outraged sensibility that she wore when Marek was about. And, as for the butterfly collector: 'He is killing these butterflies! This is *not good*. This the Tibetans will *not like*!'

'What will he do with these butterflies?' she demanded of Marek.

'He makes swap. Also, he will give the collection to the town where he lives. He is a farmer, with an orchard.'

'Apples,' said Alois unexpectedly, through his beard. 'Mushrooms.'

Elena sat back on the bed and studied him, blowing a bubble with her gum. When the bubble was huge, she popped it with her tongue.

'You like these Tibetans?'

'Yes.'

The moment was over. 'Now,' said Marek, filling the room with his bonhomie, 'we will drink beer!'

We drank beer. Elena even accepted a cigarette. Zenek, shorn-headed now in a way that showed his bone structure, had acquired a little sprig of juniper, which he lit and let smoulder, and the room took on a fug. It grew dark enough for candles, so shadows played. In the midst of all the languages we spoke, in the concrete room with stained walls, we held a little soirée, then retired to our various beds.

* * *

The door. A key fumbling in the lock, then the door crashing open. At least it tried to crash, but as ever it jarred on the floor, giving us a few seconds to wake and scramble to our feet. Then the light was flicked on, and in its glare I saw the pale hotel girl's terrified face as three policemen shoved past her into the room, stars at their shoulders, guns at their sides. We were in nightclothes, Sean and me, T-shirts and underwear. The police filled the room; the main man had a cigarette hanging from his lips, an overcoat with epaulettes slung from his shoulders, like he had watched too many movies. The girl stood in the doorway, paralysed with fear.

Then all the men were shouting, the police in Chinese. Sean, taller by a good head, physically much broader, was bawling back, 'Fuck off! Just fuck off!'

'Papers!' they demanded. 'Passports!'

'Just get out!'

By a lewd gesture they demanded to know if we were sleeping together.

'Fuck off!' roared Sean.

They shouted for a while more, then thrust us back into our room with a signal to stay there, and hauled the door closed.

We heard commotion in the corridor. More shouting, a door banging, but then they were gone. Just putting the wind up us, the foreigners. Letting us know we'd overstepped some mark. In due course we slept.

In the morning, we found a torn-off sheet of purple paper shoved under our door. It showed a hasty drawing in biro of a mountain and a strange tree and a huge jagged sun, and the words 'See you!'

We ran down the corridor at once. Elena's door was wide open and already the hotel girl was sweeping out the room. The girl didn't even glance at us as we entered. On the mattress lay a couple of pairs of knickers, some colouring pencils and a few loose pages of a book Elena had been translating, something about occult religions. I gathered up those things.

There was a fresh stain on the wall, as though tea had been thrown. The room seemed lighter, somehow. With her back to us, the hotel girl swept up a few stray dark hairs, dog hairs, some sunflower-seed husks. I wanted to say something to this young woman, by touch or gesture. She'd been so scared, what with the police and their guns. 'She's nice,' Elena had reported. 'It is difficult for her.'

We took the hint and left too. Besides, there were no strikes now, not any more. Before we went I walked up the hill by the monastery to a low summit where a collection of prayer flags fluttered, tied to sticks. I was wearing an old yellow silk scarf, which I took off and tied among the bits of cloth. What for? For the students in Beijing. For the whole damn mess. For the suffering world. How long did that scarf last, I wonder, till its last thread was shredded and blown away?

Some squares of white paper were tumbling along the grass and wildflowers by my feet, goodness knows where from, there was no one else around. I caught one as it fluttered past. It showed a little printed picture, red on white, of a winged horse rearing through the air. I kept it. It seemed a fair swap: a silk scarf to stay, a wind horse to go.

* * *

High on the plateau, at about ten thousand feet, lies a vast, shallow salt lake so large you can't see the far shore. Lake Quinghai. In different languages, Chinese, Tibetan, Mongolian, it is called 'green lake' or 'blue lake' or 'teal lake.'

We went there, a sixty-mile bus ride from Xining. The lake, cupped among low grassy hills, was large and still enough to shimmer in the breeze and, in the evening light, pink mirages wavered on its watery horizon. A sharp northern wind blew small waves ashore, a wind that had crossed Mongolia.

All around were low hills, a seemingly endless rumpled land. Late snow lingered on distant summits. Again, this was grazing country. In folds in the hills, lines of smoke rose from nomads' yurts. Sheep and yaks were white and brown dots on the hillsides. Sometimes a shout reached us, as a herd called to keep the flock in check.

There was a lakeside settlement called Heimahe, just a few flat-roofed roadside shacks and stores and telegraph poles beside the unmetalled road. At a little hostel or truck stop there, we took rooms. It was a place given to rain; deep cloud-reflecting puddles had formed. Heavy trucks passed through and, at the roadside, women sold carp caught in the lake, holding them out to the passing trucks. If a police vehicle or an official vehicle bounced into view, they hid the fish behind their backs and affected nonchalance.

It was good to be out of town. From the settlement, a short path led down to the lakeside. There, from among the sparse grasses of the shore, larks rose singing, and wildflowers grew between salt-crusted pebbles. The scent of the flowers was so strong it burned your nose.

Also at the shore was a row of eight *chorten* made of prickly juniper wood lashed together with white wool. The evening we arrived, I watched a lone monk arrive at the shore to meditate. First he made a burned-barley offering at a cairn of stones, then he settled himself cross-legged on the ground, and began reading, part chanting, from a book of scripture on his lap. The book was long and thin. He had a bowl, made of a human skull.

It was here we met Elena again. This we hadn't expected, but when I went back to the hostel there was Sean, grinning, walking across the courtyard with Elena by his side. We met with whoops of delight. We'd been worried. But 'It was nothing,' she shrugged. The police had just threatened and shouted and insisted she leave town on the first bus.

'So I came here!'

Gravely, in the half-light of another grubby room, I handed Elena the drawing pencils and pages, a precious burden, and she thanked me, but at the underwear she smiled. Dark blue, no-nonsense knickers. 'Now this I really missed!'

A clean river ran down from the hills here, one of many that fed the lake. Inland from the road it meandered in a deep channel between grassy banks before finding its way to the shore. Bright yellow wagtails prissed about on its bank, a merganser swam.

Elena and I walked beside the river. The cooling sky was tinted with wisps of mauve reflected in the slow water. Sean had gone into the clear light with his camera. There was a high-altitude expansiveness in the sky and a cool sense that summer was over, although no one knew it yet. A thumbprint of rainbow in the west. White mountain peaks.

'What will you do now?' she asked. It seemed we were in a mood to exchange confidences, now we were unobserved, in the peace of the hills. I told Elena I had made this long trip, this strange adventure, to escape a hasty marriage. Now I had to go home and face the disappointments and anger, the financial mess. I had to see my husband and seek his agreement to part. We couldn't go on. That much had become clear to me.

'Then you will be happy,' she said, simply, walking at my side. I hoped so, because I hadn't been, and neither had he.

'And what about you?' I asked.

'I will perhaps go to India. But Lhasa is my home.'

'Not Italy?'

'No. In Italy I was nearly dead.'

I looked at her quickly and she laughed, with her dark sorry-merry eyes.

'What do you mean?'

'Heroin! You are surprised! Yes. Heroin. In Milan, I was nearly dead.'

We remained a couple of days more, walking into the hills. Then we left. During the last night came a storm of wind and rain, thunder and lightning over the hills and the lake. In the morning, Elena presented us with 'a box of good luck things,' as she called it. A little box containing an aniseed, a few inches of striped Tibetan ribbon, two pressed flowers, a piece of incense.

We went back to Xining, and from there turned for home.

* * *

In the late winter of that same year, or very early the next, when I had parted from my then husband and

was living in a rented room in Edinburgh, I received a
postcard via my parents' address.

The parents, the unthought of. I am old enough
now to feel for all those parents: of the State-murdered
students, of those lost to heroin, of those who wander
off and never come home.

The card was from the country still then known as
Czechoslovakia. There, student demonstrations had
escalated to involve the workers, had become a general
strike, had swollen into a mass movement. Half a
million people had filled Wenceslas Square – we saw
all this on TV. Then came the fall of the Communist
regime of forty years.

The card was from Zenek. It was one of his own
absurdist photographs. A man with elaborate paper
wings strapped to his arms was about to take a step off a
kerb. At the bottom he'd written 'We are learning fly!'

Sean became a film cameraman, working in sometimes distant and difficult locations. He has a family
now. We never saw Elena again, but I still think about
her now and again, especially when I feel helpless, as
when news comes of some new outrage in the suppres-
sion of Tibet, or of yet another atrocity elsewhere in the
world. Recently a spate of self-immolations spread to
Labrang/Xiahe. There are pictures on the Internet of a
body in flames by the monastery wall. Of monks rising
in protest, soldiers on the streets.

'Only when we have been heartbroken can we be
truly happy' was almost the first thing she said to us.
Visualise the sentient beings who are without happiness.

Determine to place them in joy. Think – May they be happy.
Maybe it's a fully worked out spiritual position, tenable
for a student of Tibetan Buddhism, for a recovering ad-
dict, for one reincarnated from the almost-dead into a
state of willed joy.

And the art students, barely out of their teens. I
regret I didn't learn their names, or begged or bought
one of their sketches, because I have often thought
about them, too. They said they were fighting the
government with beauty. 'Do you understand?' Elena
had demanded of Marek, who doubtless became one of
the half-million people filling Wenceslas Square. *The
government will fall!*

Do you understand?

Elders

UNDER THE PLASTIC LID, a tundra landscape, as seen from the air. Blooms of bottle green, circlets of paler green, of fawn.

'Dad!' I said. 'You can't eat this. Why in god's name won't you keep it in the fridge?'

My father is shrinking. He leans on a stick.

'Why don't you eat them when we bring them? On the same day?'

Down the toilet went several small, once-nutritious portions. We are good daughters, my sister and me. Trying to be. We've taken to bringing round food because, we insisted, a daily bowl of soup and the innards of a white bread roll are not enough.

My dad's bungalow is comfortable. He can afford – we can afford – to keep it heated. He has been widowed for a decade and, before that, he was chief carer for my mother following her stroke. Hence the move to within a couple of miles of me and my then-young family. We weren't going anywhere, not then, so my parents moved close.

Friends say it's a good arrangement. Not having to do state visits. Not having to drive half-roads across the country every weekend.

Round the corner, out of sight, I text my sister: 'At Dad's. Just chucked all that food we brought, trying not to boak.' Later, I confess, I shouted at him: 'Dad, what are we to do?' He snapped back, 'Just leave me to my own devices.'

On the Friday, two friends arrive to collect me. We're going north for a long weekend. They are both older than me, retired, and skilled and competent hillwalkers. I think they're glamorous. One of their chief hill-sports is to receive the slightly patronising comments of men, then turn the conversation to reveal that they have both done all the Munros, and even climbed Himalayan peaks. Both were widowed quite young, for very different reasons.

Into the car go boots, ice axe, walking poles, and myself bearing another small dish of mashed potato.

'Can we stop at my father's, so I can nip in?'

'Of course!' they say. One of the two recently lost her own mother, who had been very elderly and confused.

* * *

Forests and peatbogs and abrupt snow-shining mountains. Buzzards on tilting telegraph poles. Passing places. Snow and deer creeping down to the roadside, because it was February, still winter. We have hopes of climbing Ben Loyal. We stay with friends in their cottage, where a peat-fired Rayburn warmed the wood-panelled rooms.

In the evening, the talk ranges over land ownership and politics and life-choices. Housing, or getting round to thinking about it. How and where it's best to live, now they were retired. What was affordable. If you were able to make choices. We all know people who are now in their seventies, still with parents alive. People who will never know life without a living parent until they are elderly themselves.

'We should live together in a commune,' someone suggests. Yes, we should.

The forecast is not great, but we go anyway, for a look-see. In a deserted farmyard we gear up, and from there begin walking to the hill over land which is boggy, reedy, heathery. The hill is clear of cloud, its complex snowy summits bright against cold blue sky. Though not a Munro, the hill looks high, rising alone from the moor. Its summits come and go, out of the cloud.

But the sky soon darkens and a squall drives down the glen. The three of us fan out, hunched, battered on our right shoulders by sleet, each picking our own way among bog-pools, thinking our own thoughts. None of us likes chatterboxes on the hill. We enjoy the freedom of our own interiority. The squall passes, we gather to cross a river by a ford. Then the land climbs steeply and we follow a burn up toward a low ridge. It's heavy going and the snow-field above looks like it might be wind-honed, icy. Soon the sky darkens again and a fresh squall drives in.

Now we're glancing at each other, laughingly. Who will speak first?

We descend back to the car, peel off gaiters and coats and muddy boots, enjoying ourselves.

I trust these women deeply, who are older than me. As we drive back down to the Kyles of Tongue, I feel free to voice what I'd been thinking about of late, out of this phase of my life. I tell them I feel as if I have a window of opportunity, but it is closing fast. No, rather I feel it has barely opened at all, because I'm being delivered straight from childcare to eldercare, without passing 'Go.' And the day job, of course.

But this is my chance, or should be. My own health is good, the kids are grown. Soon they might even be making their own money. My husband is older than me and he's fine for now, rich with his own interests and happy to wave me off on adventures; but give it a few more years...

Life has been good to us.

'Chance for what?' they ask.

'I can't actually say. But sometimes I think about going on a gap year, backpacking. Or sailing south, somehow, through the tropics. Somewhere out of Scotland! Get a sense of the majesty of the world.'

'Do it!' they urge. 'Before your joints give out!'

I'm not sure I can imagine it. Anything can happen, as we all know. Life can turn on a sixpence. The walking axe I'd brought was my mother's. She'd used it before the stroke. She was sixty. Had she ever felt free? She was the only child of a single parent who needed a lot of help.

We congratulate ourselves several times on making the right decision, in retreating from the hill.

'Imagine the headlines,' the others say. "Pensioners rescued from mountain blizzard!"'

'"Old ladies"!'

'Speak for yourselves,' say I.

* * *

I nip round to Dad's the next day. 'Well, did you eat your tatties?'

'Aye.'

'Good. You know, there's a company that delivers frozen meals ... small portions. You could give that a try, too.'

* * *

Two months passed, to the day. The late snow was gone, the daffodils were in bloom and Dad was in his chair where he often sat, next to the table with the chair turned toward the window so he could see the railway through a gap between houses. He watched the trains pass, noted their numbers. He had a dram at his elbow and also on the table lay his notes and letters in his neat handwriting. It was the morning. A kindly neighbour had called us to say she was concerned because his milk was still on the step.

The milk was on the step, and oh, we all agreed, wasn't that the best way? Everyone, everyone said it. That's the way to do it. Isn't that the best way? In your own chair at home. Who wouldn't want that? Och, he even got to finish his whisky.

Voice of the Wood

So you've really gone and done it this time you are lost in the wood how did that happen? The crazed Scots pines camped all around and blaeberries beneath and bracken shrivelled because it's October and you stand hearing nothing, the non-sound of one leaf dropping to join its siblings on the ground.

You stand still. Behind each tree, more trees. Above: glimpses of bone-white sky.

You stand. The Scots pines arrange their great limbs with no heed of you. They are weighty but also like breath on a winter morning, but it's not winter yet. Pines, and also birches, cold yellows aflame. The young birches are fragile, as though the first wind would send all their leaves fainting at once, but there is no wind.

How lost is lost?

You are not lost. You followed your map. There is a path – there is always a path through the wood; there has been since the dawn of time. The trees step aside to make one. It's a ghost trail, an animal trail maybe for deer or badgers. There are no animals, it's daytime. No wolves for sure and no bears.

You sense the woods miss the bears; they ought to be here huffing around the old trunks and berry-shrubs, but there's no huffing now. Wolves, though – the wood is old enough to remember them, just.

But you're standing in the wood, stock-still and listening and your hearing has sharpened. There fall the tiny tin-tack calls of birds foraging in the treetops, the race of water in a burn.

And now there is a moth. She appears fluttering in front of you. If this was a fairy tale she might want you to follow her, but she passes and will flatten her grey wings against the grey trunk of a tree. She has never been seen before and never will again, that was it – her sole appearance in our human world, and now it's done.

What are you doing here anyway, in the woods? Ah, well, that is the question. You wanted to think about all the horror. The everyday news – the guns, the wars, the children's tears down ashy faces, the chainsaws, the sea creatures tangled in plastic...

No, not to think about it exactly but consider what to do with the weight of it all, the knowing ... how to cope with it scroll down flick the page unplug the telly send a few quid. Really? Or take a long walk in the wood 'cause you are the lucky one and can do that, you can just shut up shop and go let the wood embrace you.

And here you are.

The trees all around, they commune with each other you can sense it, a knowingness between them. They've been rooted here centuries already and seen it all.

A plane is passing, up in the bone-white sky, above the branches and going where? Maybe over the shrinking icecap.

Concentrate.

Green ferns in the groin of an oak. Green moss cloaking a stone. Voice of a crow. Voice of a chiding wren. A smirr of rain too soft to possess a voice. Voice of the shrew, the black slug. Voice of the forest ... Did you hear something move out the corner of your eye? The same moth come back? Or another leaf falling? You are not lost, just melodramatic. The path is at your feet, see? Now carry on.

Acknowledgements

Many wonderful people made this book, giving of their expertise and knowledge, allowing me to tag along. Some have become friends, the best outcome.

Andrew Kitchener and Fraser Hunter of National Museums Scotland allowed me into the wondrous stores. Jenny Downes of Aberdeen University Museum introduced me to the Nunallaq excavation project, and in particular to Rick Knecht and Melia Knecht. I owe particular thanks to the generosity and enthusiasm of Rick and Melia. I'm grateful to Charlotta Hilderdall, and all the Nunallaq archaeologists, to Erika Larsen and of course to the people of Quinhagak, whether they be named in the book or not.

For those interested, the site blog is here:

https://nunalleq.wordpress.com/about/

On Orkney, special thanks are due to Hazel Moore and Graeme Wilson of EASE Archaeology, Westray, and all the Links of Noltland diggers, whether named or not. Some images of the site can be found here:

http://linksofnoltland.co.uk/index.html

Sandy and William McEwen of West Manse were delightful hosts. I'm grateful to Nina and Jason Wilson, and their lovely cows. In Kirkwall, I plundered the expertise of Caroline

Wickham Jones. In Stromness, there is Calum Morrison (but no more Cognac, Calum, thank you). I'm grateful to Sean Mayne Smith. And to Liz Duff and Marjory Stevens; indeed, all the climbers and 'baggers' – we go back a long way. To Freya Butler, Shona Swanson, Fergus Jamie, Duncan Butler, my love.

Yet again, Nat Jansz shared her deeply insightful thoughts throughout. I'm grateful to her and Mark Ellingham, and to Jenny Brown for her clear thinking and unfailing enthusiasm. Peter Dyer's book-cover designs are special. Creative Scotland and the Leverhulme Trust awarded funding for travel, without which the book could not have been written.

Since I began this book, my children have grown and gone out into the world, and my dear dad has passed away. So we go on. *Surfacing* is dedicated to Phil Butler, for his constancy.

Photo credits

I'm grateful to the following photographers and agencies:

Quinhagak images (pp. vi, 12, 42, 58, 75, 87) © Erika Larsen (*www.erikalarsenphoto.com*).

Reindeer Cave (p. 5) © Mike Brockhurst (*www. walkingenglishman.com*).

Scoresby's boat (p. 6) from *The Life of William Scoresby* by Robert Edmund Scoresby-Jackson.

Inuit bird purse (p. 11): photo kindly supplied by Arbuthnot Museum, Peterhead, and courtesy of Aberdeenshire Council.

Eagle (p. 100) © iStock/Getty Images.

Westray Wife (p. 105) © Carole Bumford.

Author on site (p. 106), Links of Noltland (p. 162) © Graeme Wilson.

Family photo (p. 178), author's notebook (p. 185), wind horse stamp (p. 194): author's collection.

Novice monk with author (p. 186), old woman with wind chimes (p. 209), Xiahe Fair (p. 225) © Sean Mayne Smith.

Ben Loyal (p. 236) © iStock/Getty Images.

Black Wood of Rannoch (p. 242) © David Robertson/Alamy Stock Photo.